Delicious on My Ears

The Story of Missionary John Newman

by

Marty Robinette

PRESS

OC International
P.O. Box 36900
Colorado Springs, CO 80936
www.onechallenge.org

www.xulonpress.com

Contents

Foreword

The Vietnam War—from the mid-1960s through the early 1970s, morning newspapers, evening television newscasts, and weekly newsmagazines in the United States and around the world were filled with disturbing stories and images of the terrible conflict going on in Southeast Asia which eventually claimed the lives of hundreds of thousands of combatants and civilians.

However, what the media did not report was the fact that, in the midst of the intense physical warfare, there was an equally fierce battle being waged for the souls and eternal destinies of the people living in the rugged highlands of Vietnam. For almost two decades, John and Jo Newman were at the very center of this intense spiritual struggle.

This book recounts the gripping story of how the Lord of the Harvest reconciled John and Jo to Himself through faith in Jesus Christ, then called them to leave the peaceful plains of eastern Washington state in the United States and travel halfway around the world to take the good news of the gospel of Christ to the people of Vietnam. Motivated by deep love for the mountain people and a driving passion to see them come to faith in Christ, John was involved in a diversity of missionary activities and ministries: evangelism, church planting, education, relief, and development.

In the midst of the terrible war ravaging the Vietnamese nation, the Lord blessed John and Jo's sacrificial service, along with the service of many other dedicated missionaries (some of whom were ultimately called to give their lives), to bring about a tremendous revival among the mountain people, resulting in thousands of them placing their faith in Jesus Christ as Lord and Savior.

As the current president of the mission agency with which the Newmans served for many decades, it is my privilege to highly recommend this book to you. I am confident you will be encouraged and challenged, as I was, from reading the thrilling story of the ministry of this remarkable missionary couple.

Dr. Greg Gripentrog
President, OC International

Prologue

Dreaming

Spokane, Washington, 1996

The knock at the door came at 4:30 a.m. John's daughter, Barbara, sleepily asked if they were ready, and John said they needed a few more minutes. The dark, crisp morning air was filled with the chaotic music of robins and sparrows competing for rule of the skies. Barbara stepped inside the small two-bedroom home. Getting up at 3:30 a.m. to make the 6 a.m. flight to Los Angeles might have seemed too early to most folks at that time, but John had it stuck in his mind to always arrive one hour before takeoff. Soon John and Jo were ready and were loading their two suitcases into the car. The ride to the airport was a blur. John couldn't stop his mind from racing ahead to his anticipated destination. He had rehearsed this a thousand times in his mind over the past three years. He couldn't wait to see the faces of the people he had left without saying good-bye in April of 1975. Getting on that flight meant he would truly fulfill his dream of twenty-three years: the chance to see his people once again.

When they arrived at the airport it was still dark. He and Jo were traveling light, carrying two suitcases of clothes and a briefcase of important papers and computer disks for the tribal people. They would make the morning trip from Spokane to LA and then on to Vietnam. John had to make sure a host of details were in order before this trip. His random style was an obstacle to getting all the details down. He tried to think of everything, but there was a nagging sense that he was likely to forget something important. Momentary panic attacks were quieted by short, silent prayers to the Lord. John had made the trip to Spokane International many times before, but this time he was more nervous and excited than all those times put together. He knew that this trip to Vietnam was the trip of a lifetime, a trip he and Jo had thought would never happen for them. A trip that wasn't absent risk, either.

John and Jo headed to United Airlines 727 at Concourse 5. The check-in was easy, and they were on their way. Checking through the screening machine seemed merely symbolic. They had nearly a 45-minute wait before they boarded, however. John's sister Dorothy came around 5:30 to see them off. She knew how much this trip meant to them. Sunlight was still a long while off, and simple conversation passed the time. They got their first boarding call, and their seats were first to board. Their dream was about to become reality. The months and months of anticipation and unexpected delays were finally past, and now they were on their way. John and Jo were thanking the Lord for this opportunity to see the fruit of their ministry and the love of their lives. John and Jo had experienced so much together. They suffered together the cruelties of war, and also the joys of a spontaneous outpouring of the Holy Spirit that led to revival in all the mountain tribes of Vietnam's Central Highlands.

Over twenty years earlier they had been yanked away from the country they had grown to love and were forced to leave friends they had made over twenty years of service. It was a heartbreaking experience, and they were not even able to say good-bye. Since their escape from Vietnam they had received bits and pieces of news from the tribal people of the Central Highlands. Much of the news was exciting. Thousands had come to know the Savior in spite of the communist government's attempt to snuff them out. Thousands had sat by their radios and listened to the strong and self-assured voice of John Newman, missionary and friend to the mountain people, through his weekly broadcasts. John and Jo had also heard many sad stories of brothers and sisters in the Lord being imprisoned for their faith, and some hunted down and killed by the communists.

The years of not knowing how their people were doing would soon be over. They now had a chance to meet face-to-face their friends and see the little ones who had huddled around them years ago, now grown up with their own families. It would be the greatest thrill that they could imagine. These had been the thoughts and dreams of John and Jo Newman for the past twenty-three years. John watched Jo settle into her seat. He knew she was as excited as he was, but neither of them showed it much. They were used to the Lord doing wonderful things. Not that they took them for granted, but they came to know that the Lord was in the business of blessing people.

The flight was smooth and the breakfast adequate on their three-hour trip to LA. After a short layover they boarded the plane to Ho Chi Minh City, formerly known as Saigon. The long trip would stop in Hawaii for an hour and then go on to Ho Chi Minh City by evening. They were tired, but charged with an extra measure of energy because their dream was about to come true. The entire flying time seemed to be but seconds. To greet the people of the mountains for the first time in over twenty years, when they had assumed they would never see them again, was a thrill and made the time fly by.

Though they had never cared for the thick, humid air of Saigon, they were going to welcome it like an old friend. As they circled the city they saw the red flags with the distinct yellow star flying on almost every building. Communist troops could be seen in patrols all over the city. John and Jo suddenly began to sense their hearts race in anxious fear that their presence might not be as welcome as they had come to hear. If officials did any serious background check on the passengers they would find out that John once had a close relationship with the U.S. military and in their minds stirred up trouble among the mountain people. One of John and Jo's greatest concerns was whether they could come to Vietnam without the fear of any reprisals for their work with the mountain people during the war. They also feared reprisals of some sort against the friends they planned to visit. The latest word they had seemed to indicate that everything would be OK. After all, that's why they decided to come.

Before the plane came to rest they looked out their window and saw three armored troop carriers racing toward the plane. As the airplane landed and came to a stop everyone was instructed to stay seated. The cabin door opened, and they heard muffled talk among the flight crew and the soldiers. John wondered if it could have anything to do with them. His heart began to pound heavily, and he hoped that he wouldn't hear them announce his name. He knew that his name was not spoken among the communists in friendly terms during the war, but this was years later. So much time had passed, and this was a new era. "They couldn't possibly care that I am coming back," he thought. Then a small Vietnamese officer appeared at the front of the passenger area and shouted out in a stern, high-pitched voice in broken English, "Mistare Newman ...?"

... At that point John opened his eyes to realize he was still sitting in his swivel chair in his basement office. The comfort of his chair must have overtaken him, and he had slipped into a common daydream about his desire and hope of returning to Vietnam. The hope of making it to Vietnam was constantly on his mind.

As reality began to return to his mind it underscored the depth of his desire to return to the people that God had sent him to and the people who were the love of his life. It was then that he began to muse on his entire life. Now in his latter years, he began to flash back to where this adventure all began and how the Lord had called him to a life of great fulfillment. The Lord of the universe had reached down and taken pity on this guy from Spokane, Washington, and had a special plan for his life, a plan that would take him around the world to meet and speak to thousands about the love of Jesus. The thought of God Almighty directing all this made him humble and grateful to have lived such a life.

As he began to reflect, he kept going further back in his life to the time of his childhood ...

Chapter 1

Every Knee Shall Bow

Every Christian has a unique story about how they came to Christ. Some came to the Savior early in their elementary years, some in their teens, and others later in their adulthood. Regardless of when someone comes to Christ, it remains a miracle that any of us see the light and follow Him. John Newman's story is not unlike many who came to Christ early in their adulthood. What is unique is the life that followed that important point of decision. In order to fully appreciate the life this man has lived in extraordinary service to the Lord and shared with his wife, Jo (whom he affectionately calls Josephine), we must see the drama that led to that point of repentance.

John was born in 1915 and grew up in the medium-sized city of Spokane, located in eastern Washington. Growing up in Spokane wasn't particularly easy for John and his three sisters. The family had a modest income and had a difficult time settling down in one place within the city. John moved to six different grade schools in his first eight years of schooling. His father, who worked at a local department store for twenty-seven years, would rent homes but didn't settle into purchasing a home until John was in the ninth grade in a small suburb of Spokane called Millwood.

The kids didn't really know why their dad moved so often, but usually accepted it with a stoic resolution. The last move was the most dramatic for John, who was emerging as a good athlete at his school. He was good at football and basketball, and in baseball was known in the school as the kid who could pitch a curve so good it would make Ted Williams flinch. An exaggeration, maybe, but his reputation was building and it was of extreme importance to a 14-year-old. Worse than moving and having to re-establish his reputation was having to leave his first love—a pretty blond-haired girl in his class. He was "truly smitten," he remembers. He recalls that day vividly, saying, "It was a sad day saying farewell to this girl. Boy, I had it bad. I thought it was the end of the world." The anguish of that parting stayed with him for some time. Such was the love of a 14-year-old.

Perhaps with a slight bitterness toward his father about this frequent relocation, John had to carve out his reputation as an athlete someplace altogether new. He did, however, finish out the year at Millwood Elementary, having a great time playing sports. It didn't take long to recapture his athletic prowess.

He entered ninth grade at West Valley High School and finally got over the "little blond-haired girl" and moved on to other blonds, and brunettes. Life was good for the "big man on campus." He loved his popularity and thrived on the school activities.

John's parents were Christians and attended the Christian and Missionary Alliance Church in Spokane. Like many kids, John felt forced to go to church and really didn't feel it was something he wanted for himself. He says when he got a little older (about 14 years old) he got wiser on how to get out of going to church. "I weathered some pretty hot evangelistic services in those days," he says. To be honest, he didn't want any part of Christianity. It was something that was simply getting in the way of having a good time. It wasn't just hostility toward "church," but the whole "Jesus" thing seemed irrelevant. His hostility toward the gospel grew as he got older, to the point where he remembers that he would walk on the other side of the street just to avoid those "odd" people.

Of course peer acceptance was a big thing then, as it is now. John didn't want anyone to know he was a "church-goer," so he began to run around with the "in" crowd and do what the "in" crowd did. One day he and a friend went downtown to see a W. C. Fields movie (which was considered a major sin in those days). He recalls the movie as being riotously funny, so much so that they fell off their seats. After the show he and his friend were walking down the street and decided to light up a cigarette. With a cigarette hanging out of his mouth and the match just beginning to touch the end of the cigarette, he looked up over the white protrusion in his mouth to see his mother standing three feet away with the pastor's wife. John's symbolic rebellion hanging out of his mouth was no secret anymore. Neither was his humiliation. No hole was to be found nearby to crawl into. So he stood there for a few moments, said little, and walked away with his friend thinking of all the dumb luck.

The wild days of John Newman were not over yet. In fact, they were just getting started. Sometimes the Lord's call on one's life is first recognized when the running away starts. John was forced to move again, back to Spokane, where he attended North Central High School. Another one of those moves. He quickly established himself among his peers as a lucky transfer to the school because of his athletic talent. But John was a rebel from the Lord, and he found himself in all kinds of trouble in those days.

During his senior year of high school John's family moved back to Millwood, but he finished his high school days at North Central High. He recalls an incident, representative of many of his troubled days, when he and a few buddies attended an opening of a major stretch of east Sprague Avenue where a "street dance" was held. (Only grandmothers and grandfathers would recall such an event.) His friends brought with them a bottle of "moonshine" whiskey. A risk for high schoolers, but even more so in the dry days of the early thirties. Also in attendance at the dance was the "dry squad" (the police force specifically targeting Prohibition violations). Their goal was to catch vile offenders of the Prohibition Act. John and his "rascal" buddies' goals were in direct opposition to the dry squad's.

As they were hiding back a bit from the crowd, taking their swigs from the bottle, it came to John for his turn. He tipped the bottle up, then down, and just as he put it to his side one of the guys yelled, "COPS!" John hurriedly stuck the bottle as inconspicuously as possible in his leather jacket, up under his arm, and assumed a not-guilty position. Which in reality looked conspicuously guilty.

The small crowd of friends stood nervously by as they each were frisked. One by one they were approached as each tried with all their might not to open their mouths and breathe any incriminating evidence. As the dry squad officer approached John, their nervousness increased, and all eyes were going back and forth to one other with desperate but unintelligible messages. As the officer gruffly reached inside the jacket his hands grabbed hold of the bottle and his stern eyes looked into John's. All of a sudden John was mindful of his heritage. His mind quickly flashed on the fact that he was the "son of the treasurer of the Alliance church for the past seventeen years, son of parents who would not allow cards into the house, or dancing or movies, and son of faithful churchgoers," and then he heard these heart-stopping words: "Son, you're under arrest."

His heart was pounding out of his chest. He was wondering what this would mean—"You're under arrest." How much time in jail? What is jail like? What will my parents do? How will this affect my future? Who will find out? Will it be in the papers? It was overwhelming. But it turned out not to be as major an event as he imagined. John and his friends spent no time in jail, but they were forced to confront their parents with their abhorrent activity. A punishment in itself, but not enough to turn his life around. The rebellion continued into his days after graduation from North Central in 1932. Those few years after graduation afforded less scrutiny from his seemingly overly righteous family members. He saw it as a nice relief from that pressure.

John married shortly after graduation and lived in Millwood with his wife, Josephine. He worked evenings at the paper mill in Millwood. He spent those days collecting his check, spending it, and having a good time by the standards of the world. But all was not well with John's life of independence. His mother was praying faithfully for her wayward son, and you know how that goes. Something was going to happen sooner or later.

That something turned out to be Earl Gulbranson. Earl came to Spokane for a series of old-fashioned tent revival meetings the summer John turned 21. Gulbranson was a strong, tall Norwegian man from Minnesota who had preached for some time in Montana. He was given the nickname the "Montana Cowboy." He had stayed with the Newman family earlier in John's life, and John recalled him distinctly. This gentleman was a man for the Lord, and yet he was also a strong man's man. Christianity was no sissy religion for this guy. When John heard he was coming to town he had a funny feeling deep down in his gut. Was this a conspiracy? Was his family going to trap him? He didn't know, but he still had this unshakable feeling knowing this man was coming to town.

When the tent was raised and the seats arranged near an open field by the community church, the faithful would arrive at 6:30 every morning to pray for the lost souls of their families and friends. John's mother, father, and three sisters would jump into the car and race down to the tent to pray for John and other loved ones every morning. Somehow John knew about this effort on his behalf. This knowledge led him to extra efforts to find excuses not to come to any of the meetings. He conveniently had to work most of those evenings at the mill. He made sure there was some legitimate reason for not coming to the tent. This worked for the entire two weeks of the evangelistic meetings. His avoidance tactics had worked. He was off the hook, he thought. He did not attend one meeting, and soon the pressure would be off and he could relax—except for one thing.

John's wife, Josephine, and a friend they used to double-date with, Mona Clark, decided to go to the last tent meeting to see this Montana Cowboy preacher everyone was talking about. After hearing the songs and the rousing and very convincing presentation of the gospel, the two women decided that they must give their life to Christ. They enthusiastically went forward at the invitation and became "new creations" in Christ that very night.

That night John had to work the graveyard shift at the mill, starting work at 1 a.m. Usually he would try to sleep before his shift, but that evening he lay wide awake on his bed. He knew Jo would be home soon and was anxious to talk a bit before he had to report for work. When Jo and her friend came in from the evangelistic meeting all excited and talking about something, he was afraid he knew what that excitement was all about. "They have gotten some of that 'religion,'" he thought. But at least the evangelistic meetings were finally over and this newfound enthusiasm would die down soon. However, the "rascals," as John called the meeting organizers, decided to have another week of meetings. Most likely the result of those morning prayers of Mom, Dad, sisters, and thirty-four other prayer warriors. So all of a sudden he had to conjure up a another whole week of excuses. It was getting tiring.

John was able to avoid the meetings for another week until Friday night. Somehow that night he was compelled to be there. He can't explain it to this day, but somehow he was there. Maybe it was out of a little curiosity, or he was tired of making excuses and perhaps this would pacify those who were so concerned for his spiritual welfare. "I don't remember at all what the man said except I was miserable. There was such enormous conviction of sin upon me—it was stupendous," he said of that night. He felt the presence of God, the power of God, and the majesty of God as he sat there quietly in the back-row bench of the tent.

It was an almost eerie pull on his life that he had never felt before, and it made him afraid. Afraid that this would drastically change his life and that he would have to become one of those "odd people" he had so long disdained. John was about to allow the change in his life that comes from Jesus Christ taking control of one's life. He later would be asking thousands to make that same decision. The invitation song was begun and an impassioned appeal for people to come forward to get their lives right with the Lord was made and repeated, and repeated again. John was contemplating whether to get out of his seat, but he quickly talked himself out of that step. As the final chorus to the altar call song was sung, John was glued to his seat. He was not going to go forward. He was not going to play their game. He was not going to succumb to this psychological pressure.

As the people filed out he went with them, silently bearing the oppressive call of God upon his soul. As soon as he stepped out of the tent the oppressive feeling immediately left, and the misery was gone. He noticed how the very fact of being outside the tent seemed to change completely how he felt. It was odd, but he didn't allow himself to dwell much on it at the time. He quickly began to joke around with some of his peers he met outside the tent. The pressure was gone, and it wasn't that bad. Maybe everyone would leave him alone now, he thought. But he knew something powerful had just happened. Something undeniable.

Saturday night came. It was the last night of the extended meetings and John again found himself in the tent. He really didn't know why he was there. Perhaps somehow he was deeply attracted to this misery he had felt in the tent. There was truth in the misery. There was healing in the misery. There was life in the misery. Why was he miserable? John calls it deep conviction of sin, but what did that really mean? John was coming face-to-face with the God of all creation in those moments, and he knew it. He came face-to-face with the truth that he had been running away from God for a long time. John realized his arrogant rebellion against God, and he was shamed. All of a sudden the "Man upstairs" was someone who was much closer and more personal. He was speaking to John's heart. Not only did John sense how much he had offended the Almighty, but he sensed the deep love and mercy that awaited him if he would simply surrender his life to Him. John seemed to hear for the first time the simple message of the gospel. He had heard it thousands of times before, but he never "really" heard it. All of a sudden the truths about Jesus coming to this earth to die for his sins and the offer of eternal life seemed so real and fresh.

As the meeting came to a close and the final verse to the invitation song was sung, not a soul went forward. In fact, not a soul came forward all week long. Earl Gulbranson was distressed at this lack of response, and he quickly left out the back of the tent to be alone. It was a strange ending to an overall fruitful effort. Mona was sitting next to John and suggested that he go talk to Earl outside. "What about?" John asked, and Mona retorted, "You know."

So John went out the back of the tent and saw Earl sitting on the porch of the nearby church. They began to talk, and

Earl told John his personal testimony about coming to Christ while in the Army. The details were fascinating to John, and he realized that the transformation that Jesus wanted to make in his life would be a vast improvement over the proud man John was making himself. Earl invited him to kneel and pray right there, and to invite Christ into his life and surrender to Him. But John said, "No, I have to do it coming down the aisle of the tent in front of everyone." So they walked back to the tent and a few were left, still talking and praying for John. He told them that he was going to go forward the next morning at the church service which would be held at the tent. Everyone was excited about what God was about to do in his life.

When he arrived at the tent that next day for the worship service it seemed that everyone in the whole place knew what John had said. The rebel was about to submit. The songs were sung, the message given, and the invitation song in conclusion was finished, and he was still in his seat. The misery was there, but the fight for his soul was not yet over. Deep inside he sensed time was running out. He even worried that the call on his life might begin to fade out of respect for his unwillingness. But in spite of that he backed out of his promise and refused to go forward. He thought he might go again for the Sunday evening service. He left the tent that morning an unchanged man.

That day he received a call from the mill to come to work that night. No evening service for him now. However, sensing time was running out for this decision, he and Jo made a desperate attempt to try and get someone to change shifts with him so he could go to that evening's service. He tried everyone he could think of, but no one was available. His last chance was a coworker nearby in Pasadena Park. John didn't have his number but knew where he lived, so he drove over to his house that afternoon. This was his last hope. He got out of his car and walked up to the doorstep. He rang the doorbell several times, and no answer. Dejected, he walked back to his car, and as he was opening his car door to leave, the man called out from his house and soon agreed to make the change.

John found himself back in the sawdust-covered floor and the musty scent of canvas, attending that evening's service. The man talked, but John doesn't recall any of the words. In fact he wasn't really paying any attention. He was having this internal conversation with the Lord and with himself. It was a wrestling match within his soul. The decision he faced was the most important one of his life. The battle for who would rule his life was intense. Would he surrender to Jesus Christ and allow him to rule and guide his steps, or would he decide to rule his own life? The words of the preacher were not important at this point. They were dwarfed by the soft and firm words of the Holy Spirit in his mind.

John had heard it all before anyway. The gospel was no stranger to him. What was different was how real and personal it all was now. Jesus' love for him was present and incomprehensibly powerful. His sacrifice on the cross made sense and was intensely personal because John was seeing himself through the eyes of God. His need to surrender his entire life was becoming more attractive every minute. To make that step from being lost in misery and sin to the other side where there is forgiveness and joy was the only reasonable response. The songs were sung, the message preached, and the invitation song "Just as I am, without one plea" was sung until finished. John was still in his seat. It seemed as if he were frozen there.

The song leader knew that John had said he would come forward, and when he didn't, he decided to give John some more time and started another invitation song, "Softly and tenderly Jesus is calling, calling for you and for me." The words of that song seemed as if they were written just for him. "Jesus is calling ... for me." How could he resist such

an invitation as that? he thought. As the song approached
the final chorus John was determined to keep his word to
Earl Gulbranson, the Montana Cowboy, and his parents to
come forward. As he began to move his leg to the aisle he
found he still couldn't move. His leg weighed a ton. He took
a deep breath and tried again with all his might and finally
got that first leg to move. He stood up and walked slowly.
He began to weep quietly. It surprised him. He had held back
his tears for almost anything for years. No physical pain had
been able to cause him to cry, nor any touching emotional
experience. He was a man, and men don't cry. But now the
weeping turned to sobbing and he didn't care.

The conviction was heavy and painful, but the remedy
was sweet as the final words of the chorus were resounding
in this newly created soul:

Come home, come home,
Ye who are weary, come home;
Earnestly, tenderly, Jesus is calling,
Calling, O sinner, come home!

John knelt down with his father on one side and Earl on
the other at the altar and prayed a simple prayer. The words to
the prayer were his own, and they were simple. He managed
to whisper amidst his sobbing, "Oh Lord, here is this mess of
a life. If you can do anything with it, it's yours. Amen."

That entire three weeks of meetings had brought forth
the harvest of only two souls, and that on the very last night.
Little did the Montana Cowboy know that this one man
would later be used to teach, preach, and lead hundreds to
the Lord Jesus all around the world.

Chapter 2

Here I Am, Lord, Send Me

John's humble walk to the altar, with his knees trembling and the sum of his life seemingly focused on that very moment, began a tremendous change in him, a change he didn't think possible. One of the first things that happened to John was tears. A tough man's man at age 21 had begun to cry like a baby out of deep repentance and the realization of the rivers of mercy shown to him at that moment—the realization of Jesus being alive and present. All at once God had given John an insight into His ways. The truth of this profound moment had to be shared with others, and that truth had to be shared with a desperate sense of urgency.

The night of his salvation, John reported to work at the mill. He didn't go jumping around telling everyone he had "gotten saved." He simply did his job with a little more energy that night and mused on the new life he had begun. He had the graveyard shift and was too excited to sleep had he had the opportunity.

He found a strange thing happening to him. He at once gave up cigarettes and drinking, never to return. That didn't seem hard. He had expected it, almost. But what surprised him was that even his vocabulary was being altered in a dramatic way. He found that there began to be blank spaces

27

in his sentences where profane words once had filled the air. An all-new way of expressing himself was beginning to emerge in quiet testimony to a changed life.

John began to attend a Bible study and read the Bible regularly. The revolution in his soul was dramatic. Every time he would read or hear the name of Jesus he began to weep. At Friday night prayer meetings he prayed for his friends and their salvation. Heaven and hell were very real to John, and he knew that if his friends didn't hear and respond to the gospel they were doomed to an eternity of suffering and darkness. He didn't know how to pray, so he wrote their names on paper and often just wept as he considered each one.

John's intense concern for the lost began to permeate all his thinking. He was beginning to get the feeling that God had a special call on his life, that He might soon lead John to a lifetime of service in preaching the gospel and leading souls to the Savior. It was an exciting proposition, but he wasn't entirely sure. It was just the beginning, and he had a long way to go. But even at such an early point in his spiritual growth, John knew God could use him if he was willing to be used. He had begun his missionary call in his own Jerusalem, but his faithfulness would eventually call him to the uttermost parts of the earth, particularly to a tribal people few cared for or even knew existed.

It wasn't long before John knew for sure that the Lord had something special in mind for the rest of his life. John's thirst for the Word and willingness to serve were obvious to all around him. People began to mention to him that he should consider full-time service. At first he wanted to simply be a good layman, but as time went on, serving the Lord as a career sounded more attractive. That still, small voice was beginning to confirm a suspicion he had about his future.

At one time, full-time Christian service had seemed to him like the worst fate anyone could face. But as the Lord worked in his life it seemed like the best life imaginable. In 1935 the Lord called John and Jo to sell their house and move to Seattle, Washington, to attend A. B. Simpson Bible School. Simpson was the founder of the Christian and Missionary Alliance Church. It was quite a step of faith for John and Jo, because they embarked on this adventure in the heart of the Great Depression.

Humanly speaking, it was a terrible time to start going to Bible school or start a ministry. Times were tough for anyone to make it, let alone a young couple going to Bible school. The Lord provided for their needs in more ways than one. It was the beginning of God showing them that He was truly faithful. Seattle was an exciting place to be, however, because as John described it the place was abuzz with the activity of the Holy Spirit. There was an unusual effectiveness to the evangelistic efforts throughout the city. It seemed in those days that almost every evangelistic service had new believers coming forward. For a budding evangelist it was a great encouragement.

In the Bible school, the Spirit of God was working mightily as well. John recalls one day in particular when a young student went up before the rest of the school for the chapel time devotional to give his personal testimony. As he approached the podium it seemed like just an ordinary talk by one of the students, as was the custom, but what happened was not. This young man opened his Bible to Isaiah 53 and read verse 6, "All of us like sheep have gone astray, each of us has turned to his own way; but the LORD has caused the iniquity of us all to fall on Him." That's all he could say. He stood still for a few moments, then tears began to well up in this student's eyes and he became speechless. He stood still for what seemed an eternity. Everyone present knew what was happening to him. He was experiencing a deep identification with this verse, and the Lord was speaking directly to him.

As the whole school was witnessing this, the dignified president of the school likewise started to weep uncontrollably. Everyone was dumbfounded. It didn't take long until the whole student body was struck with the deep truth of those familiar words and many more began to weep. For three class periods the bell would ring, but was ignored because God was doing a great work in the hearts of those students. The entire school was spellbound by the magnitude of God's grace. One by one, people began to get up and share how those few simple words from Isaiah had touched their hearts in a new way and that they wanted to get right with the Lord. Those words showed them that they didn't have the luxury to wait around for someone else to share His Word with the world; it had to be them. Everyone seemed to identify with this thought.

That one day started something special that went on for weeks. Everyone looked forward to chapel time now, whereas before it was simply a duty. Someone would always share something new and vital that had happened or something they had learned. A mini revival was taking place in the school. It was a foreshadowing of things to come in John's ministry. God was real to these young men and was using them in a mighty way for His glory. John was sensing the awesomeness of his personal calling to the ministry. It was a bit overwhelming at times, but he claimed the verse Philippians 4:13, "I can do all things through Him who strengthens me." He was looking forward to the excitement that this venture of life surrendered to Jesus would bring.

As the three years of Bible school training gave John a background of knowledge and doctrine, it also developed his preaching opportunities. He preached everywhere he could, from the Union Gospel Mission, to area churches, to the streets of Seattle. He discovered he had a strong speaking voice and most of all a heart for evangelism. "Those were life-changing days," he recalls. The late thirties and early forties saw many pastors, missionaries, and evangelists come through Simpson Bible School, with a multiplying effect we will only be able to know when we get to heaven. Those fellow students have had vital ministries literally all over the world.

John graduated in 1938 and set off on his first official ministry, the pastorate of the Christian and Missionary Alliance church in Longview, Washington. The varied and awesome responsibilities of a pastorate did not seem to fit John and his gifts. It was a valuable experience, but he soon felt certain that the pastorate wasn't for him.

While he was pastor in Longview, however, he accepted an invitation to hold evangelistic meetings at the community church of Ryderwood, Washington, known for having the largest lumber camp in America. Many people came to the meetings, with about three quarters of them being unbelievers. He loved preaching the good news of Jesus and the cross and saw several of those tough men come to know the Lord. It was an exciting time for John. The Lord showed him through that experience that the ministry of evangelism would be the direction for his life.

After leaving the pastorate in Longview in 1939 John continued his evangelistic ministry in the Spokane area. John and Jo made their home in Spokane and John traveled extensively throughout the area. John's gift for evangelism was soon recognized by his peers. He was ordained as an evangelist by the Pacific Northwest Evangelistic Association in those early days after Bible school. He would travel to most of the small towns in the area. John continued to claim "I can do all things through Him who strengthens me," and he saw that the Lord could use even a man such as him to bring souls to the Savior.

The words of Jesus that most often rang in his ears were some of Jesus' final words on earth: "Go therefore and make disciples of all the nations" (Matt. 28:19). Those simple and often repeated words of the Great Commission were not meant for someone else to fulfill; they were meant for him. The call on John's life was profound, yet simple; extraordinary, yet ordinary. He was simply obedient to the commands and applied them personally to his life. It is probably what all of us should be willing to do, but John actually lived it, and it led to a host of opportunities.

As he traveled about the inland Northwest region he hungered for places to preach the gospel. Any town that wanted a series of meetings, John would be there. Like any evangelist, he yearned to see many come to Christ, and if possible to be part of a true revival. In the town of Lewiston, Idaho, he recalls the closest thing to a revival he can remember outside of his work in Vietnam.

Night after night he would travel down the infamous, long, hairpin-curved, and arduous road to Lewiston known as the "Lewiston Grade." He would pray all the way down the road, first that his brakes wouldn't fail and then for the Holy Spirit to use him to reach people for Christ. Both prayers were answered. On the last night of a series of evangelistic meetings about 300 people showed up. That is a pretty large crowd for a small town, but what was incredible was that about 275 of the 300 people there that night came forward at the invitation. The Holy Spirit brought deep conviction of sin to the people's hearts. It was so great that several of the big, strapping men of that lumber and farming community were sobbing so hard that "the windows literally rattled," John recalls.

Many Christians rededicated their lives to the Lord and many received Christ. Ultimately, out of that harvest came a host of full-time ministers. Some plant, some water, but God gives the increase (1 Cor. 3:6), and what John was so excited about was that he could be one who planted or watered and could have the special privilege of seeing the increase. One time years later, in a meeting in Oregon, John met two pastors who had been converted at those meetings in Lewiston. He later learned that one convert became a missionary to Hong Kong and another went as a missionary to South America. "A very heart-satisfying thing to know," said John. "That's the way it is when you serve the Lord." He couldn't get enough of this life of service, a life that really counted and was making a difference for eternity. God was building His church, and John was a workman in the project.

Around the same time, he was traveling through the rolling wheat fields and pine-forested mountains of the inland Northwest in the late 1930s and early 1940s. He later worked his way through western Canada. John recalls these as some of the most fruitful days of his life's ministry. On one particular visit there was a major drought in the region of Saskatchewan and Alberta. The earth was so parched that the earth cracked wide open. The people even talked about a place where there was a crack so wide a horse could fall into it. Not lost in the hyperbole was the fact that the farmers of western Canada were in very difficult times, and despair was setting in.

The time seemed right to give spiritual drink to the thirsty souls of Canada. Times were still hard, and people didn't have any money to go out for entertainment. So they would come to church on Sunday evenings. The crowds would be three times larger in the evenings than in the morning services. The doors of opportunity were wide open. A fellow preacher, Herb Anderson, would go with John to these small towns in Canada to reap the spiritual harvest.

The services from 1940 through 1941 were particularly memorable due to the war going on in Europe. Canada, a part of the British Commonwealth, was already involved in the war against Nazi Germany, and many British fighter pilots trained in western Canada. The United States had not yet entered the war, but the clouds of war were beginning to be seen on the horizon. The urgency of war seemed to drive people to the churches in search of spiritual assurance. John loved being a part of the Lord's work at this critical time.

Shortly after making a few trips through the region John was called by the Christian and Missionary Alliance church in Edmonton to be the pastor. It was a tempting offer. It was a large church with a rich tradition. But John turned it down because he knew that wasn't his calling. "Those were great days; the benefits and blessings of those days have followed me all the days of my life," he recalls fondly. Places like Edmonton, Saskatoon, Marwayne, Kitscotty, and many more are the places the Lord was with John because John was with the Lord.

He recalls a reunion several years later that someone set up in Verminion. One of the laymen tried to bring together as many as were able to come who had received new life in Christ from the meetings John had held with Herb Anderson. The reception hall of the church was full, and the blessing was overwhelming. As in so many other cases, several people had gone on to do full-time Christian work around the world. The others who were there had been serving the Lord faithfully in their churches. John knew that there was always a ripple effect from leading just one soul to Christ. To see it actually happen was a thrill he remembers to this day.

In December 1941 John held a new set of meetings in Lewiston. He would travel nightly back to a small town not far from Lewiston, called Uniontown. He was staying there with his beloved sister Dorothy and brother-in-law Rolf Hansen. Rolf was a dear man and close friend who was the pastor of the Community Church of Uniontown.

Those were rough days for pastors. Rolf didn't have a car, and John recalls getting up early on Sundays to fire up the potbellied stove to get the church warm before the people arrived. Early one afternoon John was listening to a gospel radio program on the floor of Rolf and Dorothy's home when the infamous news came about the bombing of Pearl Harbor,

Hawaii, by airplanes from the Imperial Japanese Navy. "It was terrifying news. Everyone knew what that meant. We were going to be at war." There was a sinking sense of dread over almost everyone in the country. John felt it too. The war was going to change everything about life in America. The needy days of the Depression were moving to the threatening days of world war. He quietly asked the Lord that evening what he could do to serve his Savior best in this situation.

John immediately applied for a chaplaincy in the Army, but the Lord had different plans. He was denied that opportunity, but in the meantime John had become part of a singing quartet. The quartet, made up of Clay and Mary Helen Cooper, Les Schragg, and John, traveled up and down the Pacific Coast states putting on evangelistic meetings for the servicemen at their training camps.

One of the most memorable times was in 1943 when John had the opportunity to speak to 3,000 Marines in San Diego, California, one Sunday morning. There were about 1,500 men at each service. It was an open-air service and the weather, of course, was warm and clear, but the men were solemn. They knew that about 60 percent of their kind were dying in the South Pacific fighting the Japanese. These men were face-to-face with the prospect of their mortality. It made for a strange brew of bravery mixed with dread and a lot of uncertainty in these young Marines' minds.

John, knowing the awesome task of the moment, breathed a simple prayer, humbly thanking God for giving him this great opportunity to preach eternal salvation through the one and only Savior, Jesus Christ, to these brave young men. He knew and the soldiers knew that many would never return. On that morning about 1,500 young men responded to the invitation to receive the Lord into their lives. Were they foxhole prayers? Maybe. But the thief on the cross is thankful today for such an invitation.

During the war years John and Clay Cooper, a lifelong friend and fellow minister, held Youth for Christ evangelistic events in Spokane. Their most successful meetings were when they attempted to attract the many military personnel who were in the area. Thousands of soldiers were coming to Spokane at that time from Geiger Field, Farragut Naval Station, and Fort George Wright Army base.

John and Clay would arrange to block off streets in downtown Spokane and preach. It was a unique and amazing opportunity for them. People were open to the Lord, and John and Clay were ready to take advantage of the situation. This wasn't like a salesman taking advantage of a weak and unsuspecting client, but an act of love—the love it takes to boldly share one's faith so as to give true and lasting hope to someone who needs it desperately.

Out of that ministry came the desire to go overseas. Their first opportunity for such a venture was in Japan shortly after the war. John and Clay were able to secure the services of the Eureka Jubilee Singers to go with them. They were one of the most popular black gospel singing groups in America. They originated in Chicago, and their singing thrilled audiences around the country. They came to Spokane and helped John and Clay raise money for this overseas venture. John and Clay raised the money quickly and arrived in Japan in 1950 for their first evangelistic meetings overseas. It was one of the most exciting opportunities John had had up to that time.

They were greeted by Dick Hillis (founder of the missionary organization Overseas Crusades) at the airport. He encouraged John and Clay to go to other places in the Orient while they were there. Interestingly enough, what was planned as a trip to Japan ended up as a trip around the world, stopping at Taiwan, the Philippines, Thailand, Hong Kong, and India before going home by way of the Atlantic. They were deeply impressed with the exotic places of the world, full of amazing cultural traits that make them all worth visiting. But what impressed them more than all the color and exotic culture of the Orient were the spiritual needs of the people.

The people of Japan by this time were a desperate people. The whole country was groping to rebuild their shattered lives after World War II. The religion that supported them for years, known as Shintoism, played a large part in leading them into a catastrophic war. The promises of the Imperial Japanese government had failed them. They needed to rebuild on some new foundation, but the people had no real direction. John recognized that their spiritual needs far outweighed their material needs.

In Japan, John recalls, "Sometimes it wasn't clear how effective the preaching was because the Japanese would tend to do whatever you asked them to do ... They would come forward, bow, run in place, I suppose, if you wanted them to, due to the fact of our recent victory over them in World War II. It was terrible; you couldn't tell if they were sincere." However, those were days when John was chasing after every opportunity to make a difference in the lives of anyone who would listen to the gospel. The sincerity issue would be for God to know. The doors of opportunity kept opening, and John was going to go through as many doors as the Lord would allow.

Two years later, in 1952, John and company were off on another round-the-world missionary trip, this time by way of the Atlantic. First they went to France, then Portugal, and then on to the West African nation of Nigeria. John had some missionary friends there, and he wanted to stop and encourage them as well as preach. John worked with missionaries on the field from Sudan Interior Missions (SIM), the Evangelical Alliance Mission (TEAM), and the Lutheran Brethren during these tours. From Africa they made their way to Australia, Indonesia, and then on to French Indochina.

They hadn't originally planned to stop in French Indochina, which later became better known as Vietnam, Laos, and Cambodia, but John met a man named Bernard King, the treasurer for the Christian and Missionary Alliance denomination in New York City. He had helped with the team's financial matters before they left for France. Bernard King introduced them to a missionary from Indochina, and the missionary invited the Youth for Christ team to Saigon. Like many Americans of his time, John didn't even know where French Indochina was located. When the team got there, however, they found an open door for evangelism they rarely saw in other parts of the world. They visited the Mekong Delta region, then traveled north to the Central Highlands for a visit to the tribal people known as the Montagnards.

When John preached to the tribal people of Vietnam he fell in love with them. The team visited several villages near the town of Ban Me Thuot, located in the central part of what would later become South Vietnam. The villagers had nothing else to do, so they would come and listen to the American quartet sing. The preaching was translated three different times. First John would speak in English, then missionary Herb Jackson would translate into Vietnamese, then a tribal interpreter would translate from Vietnamese into the tribal language.

To say the least, there was a little punch taken out of the delivery. John recalls that when he returned years later the people actually remembered what he had talked about and what Joe Erickson of the quartet had sung. They called Joe "the little man whose voice fills the whole world." Little did John know that the chance meeting in New York with Bernard King would end up changing his life forever, giving him a passion for the heartwarming "mountain people" of Vietnam that exists to this day.

The team made its way from Vietnam back to Japan and preached in a memorable small town in the northern part of Honshu. With about three hundred in attendance, many came forward to receive the Lord, and John wondered again if they were sincere conversions. Of course there is often no way of knowing at that moment, but several were sincerely crying. He knew something was happening and later found out that from that meeting a Lutheran Brethren missionary started three new churches. As John reflected on the meeting he said, "Now that's what I call worthwhile! We got a taste of heathenism in Japan and India that I've never experienced before. It was overwhelming. It was a thrill to turn some around in the direction of the living Lord."

John's heart of concern for the spiritually lost was beginning to turn more and more to the distant shores. Burning within him was the same desire that burned in the heart of the apostle Paul when he said to the Roman Christians that his greatest desire was "to preach the gospel, not where Christ was already named" (Rom. 15:20). John wondered if he would ever have an opportunity like that in his lifetime.

Chapter 3

The Call

In the early fifties John was working through parts of Canada and the Midwest, holding evangelistic meetings. One of John's specific talents was to raise money for overseas missionary efforts. He had a way of explaining the needs of the lost souls in the world that made people hand over their money. To some of John's friends this is his greatest spiritual gift. Be that as it may, John used all of his gifts to the maximum. He would do whatever had eternal good. One of his favorite sayings was, "Only one life, 'twill soon be past, only what is done for Jesus will last." It was a lifetime passion of his to serve the Lord, and it inspired others to do the same.

While traveling through the Midwest he met some friends in Illinois, where he stayed for a few nights. While there, he received a phone message from Clay Cooper and Don Hillis that they were specifically praying that the Lord would send John and Jo overseas to the mission field. He thought at first that he was talking about Joe Erickson, who sang with John in the quartet, but they were talking about Josephine, his wife. "That was kind of shocking. You know, when someone is praying for you, you better pay attention. Maybe the Lord is getting ready to crack you over the head again," recalls John with a smile.

However, they kept praying and John kept feeling a bit nervous about the whole idea. "What is going to come of this?" he thought. It wasn't entirely logical to send a man and his wife at the age of 40 to a foreign mission field. There are all kinds of reasons that this would not be a good idea, such as the difficulty of learning a new language, and family responsibilities, and who knows what. He was trying to develop in his mind a set of reasons why such a venture would be out of the question. If he was going to go overseas for an extended period, the Lord was going to have to give him a big shove, he thought. Not that he wasn't willing, but in his mind, there had to be someone better suited than himself for such a task.

On another occasion around this time John was traveling by car from Fergus Falls, Minnesota, to Cherokee, Iowa, to speak at a missionary conference at First Baptist Church. While he was driving, he listened on the radio to the Old Fashioned Revival Hour with the legendary Charles Fuller speaking. John recalls that "he was preaching on heaven, and I didn't like it. I didn't like it one bit ... Didn't comfort me at all. That is when the Lord really spoke to me." He was traveling about 70 miles an hour (which was legal in those days), trying to get to the church in time for the evening service.

The lush farmland, a checkerboard of green and yellow, was beautiful. It stretched as far as the eye could see, but it was only a blur to John. Not because of the speed of the car, but because of his hypnotic concentration on the preacher's words. And it wasn't exactly the words of the preacher that were having such an effect, but what God was suggesting to John through those words. "I heard this man, he sounded old and tired and content. Ready for heaven and thinking that would be a pretty good place. But I thought, Oh, Lord! You can't come yet. I haven't done anything."

John was distraught about the possibility that Jesus would return before he had a chance to speak the gospel to the folks around the world who needed to hear and repent. As a result, thoughts of going out on the mission field himself were upon him once again. These thoughts were beginning to grow and take root, and more importantly, it sounded more attractive all the time.

From Iowa he made his way back to Spokane. Soon he found himself as the interim pastor of Beacon Chapel, a small community church on Spokane's northeast side. Rolf Hansen, John's brother-in-law, had taken the pastorate there and had fallen ill with heart trouble. It was 1953, and John found himself in unfamiliar territory, knowing that being a pastor was not his gift, but the Lord would likely bless just the same.

This seemingly unimportant side step in his evangelistic ministry turned out to be one of the most significant times in his life. John's heart was in missions and raising money for such causes around the globe. So he decided that this small church should do its part for world missions. The church had a tradition of emphasizing its Sunday school program and being locally minded. It had little involvement in world missions up to that point.

John began to preach on the subject of "God being a missionary." He explained that God shows His concern for the lost around the world throughout the entire Bible. The church held a missions conference and he introduced the concept of "faith promise" giving. This is a program for giving in which a person prays about the amount the Lord will supply for them to give to missions above and beyond the amount they give to the church, and then trusts God to supply that amount for the year. There was uncertainty as to how the people of the church would respond to this new idea. John sensed that it caused some concern in the people, but it could also provide the means to send more laborers into the harvest field. So he pursued the idea.

The church set a date for the faith promise pledge cards to be turned in, and the missionary budget would be set according to the total amount of dollars pledged. The tension was building throughout the church membership as Faith Promise Sunday was at hand. Soon they would see what the Lord would do. They collected the pledge cards for two Sundays. On the final Sunday they counted up the amount. Excitement filled the air, and this small, outwardly plain-looking and unattractive church with a membership of about a hundred would commit thousands of dollars to see that the gospel would go out to all the ends of the earth.

This had a near-revival impact on the church. Shortly after the faith promise offering a little old lady called Pastor Hansen and told him that she was going to retire the $700 debt the church had incurred. Glenn Johnson, later to be a missionary to Vietnam himself, was leading the junior high group, and seven of his group prayed to receive Christ within weeks of the faith promise. One of the greatest blessings for John was to see his son-in-law come forward after a worship service at Beacon Chapel to receive Christ into his life. John had the opportunity to lead him in that most significant prayer.

It was a testimony to the grace of God and how He could richly bless out of any willing vessel. John's heart broke as he saw people take God at His word and give beyond what they were able in order to fulfill the Great Commission. It was an emphasis that small church held for decades. For John, it confirmed in his mind how much God really is a missionary, and he wanted to go overseas himself just that much more.

With this step of faith by Beacon Chapel, John felt more and more that he was to make his own step of faith. John had made his own faith promise, and he felt wonderfully in the center of God's will. The Lord was talking to John in that still, small voice, saying, "You got everybody else out there. How about *you* going?" Something was going to happen to John and Jo, he knew it; it would be exciting, it would be crazy, it would be exactly what the Lord wanted them to do.

In 1953, after months of struggle in his heart about this notion of going overseas, planted there by the prayers of his friends, he stood up in a group meeting that was raising money for other mission concerns and declared, "You can believe this or not. But I'm going." It stunned everyone. Most of them thought that he meant that he would be going out on a short-term assignment. But he was talking about a definite career move. His heart was set on that small, beautifully green, remote land of Vietnam. He remembered the people of the mountains there who touched his heart, and he wondered if they would be the people to whom he would be sent.

It became clear that this was no ordinary train of thought brought on by guilt for making years of appeals for other missionaries and not going himself. He had that sinking, miserable feeling once again, reminiscent of the tent meeting when the Lord began speaking deeply to his heart. It was not altogether unpleasant, but the uncertainty and the possible magnitude of going overseas were great, particularly when you're about 40, particularly when you might be going to a hostile region wracked by war for decades.

The Lord made it increasingly clear that Vietnam was the place he was to go. With further study it became clear that this was not a peaceful land. The French had been fighting the Vietminh since the end of World War II in 1945, when they attempted to assert control over Indochina as they had before the war. The Vietminh were Vietnamese national-ists who adopted the communist ideology and were seeking independence for Vietnam. The French fought for nine years to defeat the Vietminh forces of Ho Chi Minh, with little success. The Vietminh eventually defeated the French in 1954 at a place called Dien Bien Phu, located near the northwest border of Vietnam. The French forces were leaving about the time John would arrive for his first journey as an associate missionary. The uncertainty of the times for John and Jo was accentuated by the uncertainty of times for Vietnam itself.

The political situation in Vietnam was not going to settle down soon. After Dien Bien Phu and the exit of the French, the country's future was in the hands of negotiators. The United States was a key player in these negotiations. The United States had been giving the French financial support in their attempt to defeat the forces of the Vietminh. The U.S. was greatly concerned over the threat of communist expansion in the region, as well as everywhere else in the world. In Geneva, Switzerland, in 1954, an agreement was made to split the nation in two, one half north of the 17th parallel and the other south. North Vietnam would be under the communist leadership of Ho Chi Minh, and South Vietnam would be a nationalist country under the leadership of Bao Dai, and then shortly after, under Ngo Dinh Diem. Under the terms of the Geneva Accords, there were to be free elections in both North and South Vietnam that would lead to unification. These elections, however, never took place. North Vietnamese leadership anxious to unite under one communist government soon began to support offensive military and political actions in the South to bring about this desired unity.

But John's call was there, unmistakable in his heart as well as in Jo's. They would obey. John knew the feeling all too well. There was nothing greater than being in the center of God's will and nothing more miserable than being out. No earthly pleasure, no possession, no fame or fortune could compare to the inner joy of knowing you are in the center of God's will. The chance to preach Christ where His name had yet to be heard was before John. It made no sense, and yet it made perfect sense. It was all coming together like a well-directed symphony, and the conductor was God. He would go because he was sent. It was as simple as that for John.

John made two trips to Vietnam before he settled in for a long-term commitment. They made one trip in 1954 and the other in 1955. Both trips were with the Youth for Christ quartet. Each trip was an exciting venture, and was especially enjoyable because it seemed that the Vietnamese and tribal people of Vietnam were particularly open to the gospel.

John recalls that in April 1955, during his second short-term trip with the Youth for Christ quartet, they were in Saigon and fighting broke out. The first experience with war is terrifying to anyone, and the Newmans were no exception. They found themselves held up in a missionary guesthouse. Explosions and gunfire surrounded them, and their safety was indeed in jeopardy. With bullets flying in every direction, some hitting the guesthouse, John had no idea what to do, which only added to the terror. While this was going on, John and Clay Cooper had access to a tape recorder and made a tape recording right in the middle of the firefight. The tape described the situation in great dramatic detail and was later broadcast on the radio back in the States as soon as they could get it out. This brush with death, however, did not deter the Newmans in the least.

They returned to the United States later that year to make preparations for full-time missionary work in the land of Vietnam. The Lord's leading was getting clearer all the time. This was where He wanted them to be and to stay in spite of its many dangers. They would be willing to go, and even anxious to go. Having spent some time with the mountain people, they grew to love them—the kind of love that compels one to do whatever it takes to give others the hope of eternal life in Christ. A love that a nonbeliever couldn't understand, because its origin is from God. This love would propel the Newmans to a life of dedication to the people of the land of Vietnam that continues to this day.

Preparations were made for them to go to Vietnam as career missionaries under the missionary organization Overseas Crusades in 1958. The Lord quickly added to their support, and people were excited to send these dear people to a land where many had never heard the name of Jesus.

Rolf and Dorothy Hansen took John to Los Angeles from Spokane to send him off. John was going out six months before Jo would join him. The anticipation was tremendous for both of them. John had traveled around the world three times and been on many trips, but this one was special. They both had an awareness that this ride would be the blossom of the flower that had been budding for years. Gratitude filled their hearts. The fact that they were chosen to go to this land, that they had the strength to go, that they had the desire to go, that they had the financial resources to go, and that they had the backing of many prayer warriors was humbling and exciting.

While they had a few days in Los Angeles the Newmans and the Hansens were able to have some interesting meetings with key figures of the evangelical world, such as John's good friend Cliff Barrows of the Billy Graham Crusade ministries. He had the opportunity to share their burden and new ministry with Barrows. He also had a very special meeting with evangelist Merv Rosell in Los Angeles just the day before he left. Each of these meetings proved to be most providential in the days and years to come in regard to their ministry to the people of Vietnam.

The meeting with Merv and Vi Rosell was the most extraordinary meeting. Merv was a nationally known evangelist, akin to Billy Graham until Graham's popularity grew well beyond Merv's. But he remained involved in smaller evangelistic crusades until his retirement. John and Merv hit it off and became soul brothers from that moment on.

Merv, having a lot of financial resources available to him over the years, has sent thousands of dollars to assist John and other missionaries to help the roughed-up, displaced, war-torn people of Vietnam. The money didn't go to support John personally. It was always used to assist a particular need of the people or some aspect of their ministry. John today marvels at the grace of God in that short meeting just before he left for Vietnam. If they had never met, literally hundreds of people would have suffered much more and died as a result. God used Merv Rosell in many ways and so many times, because he was extremely sensitive to the needs of the people of Vietnam. All because he met John Newman that one day in 1958.

Before the plane trip to Vietnam the Hansens and Newmans were able to go sea fishing in the Los Angeles region. John would never pass up an opportunity to fish. Rolf and Dorothy wished they had, because of the infamous "green flu" that attacks some while on the sea in a small boat. But John had a whale of a time.

The day to board the airplane to Vietnam finally came. John had been to Vietnam before, but this time it was to stay. This time it was to forge a ministry alongside of the Christian and Missionary Alliance work and to spread the gospel any way he could in Vietnam. Sleep was hard to get the night before. John was given to creating scenes in his mind of the portions of Vietnam he had already seen. He would visualize places he had visited and worked in before and would imagine what kind of work he might begin. The specifics of his ministry were vague. He would likely be establishing his own work among the Vietnamese people, the people who might only have a few years of freedom ahead of them. John was going as a humble associate at first, assisting existing work going on in the country.

John thought there might even be a chance to do pioneer work with the tribal people, to actually present the name of Jesus to people who had never heard His name before. Only God knew, and that was OK with John for now. The uncertainty made him both excited and nervous. Just before boarding the plane he experienced pangs of doubt about this being God's will, such thoughts as, "You're too old ... This is a hostile land ... How can you bring your wife to such a place? You're not trained properly ... You can't learn a new language ... It would be better to have a younger couple go instead of you ..." But soon, as he boarded, the Lord would speak softly and reassuringly to him that it was His will. Too many direct signs from God had been given along the way to ignore. Too many pieces had fallen into place. Too many answered prayers to ignore. This was the right place. This was the right time. There would be no more doubts.

As he said good-bye to Jo and the Hansens, it came to him how miraculous every day really can be, how the Lord's guiding hand in a believer's life is firm and strong when you are willing to put your hand into His. As John boarded the plane and took his seat, he thought how wonderful it was to be married to a woman with the same heart for God as his, who likewise would be willing to risk all to go to this hostile and foreign land. That she, too, was guided with the same hand of God as he. He was deeply thankful for Jo. He knew that if he hadn't had such a wife, he wouldn't be able to serve the Lord as he was.

The picture of what he would be doing was still out of focus. Many details were yet to be determined. God saw fit to make only this day clear. He was on that plane, headed for an oriental culture nearly incomprehensible to the Western mind, and that's exactly where God wanted him to be.

Chapter 4

Delicious on My Ears

John Newman, evangelist, preacher, and missionary fund-raiser, was about to land on the soil he knew God had called him to for his life's ministry. Approaching the sprawling city of Saigon, there was an excitement that could only come from God. Knowing that he would be involved in bringing these people the most important message ever given to mankind was a thrill. The year, 1958. Most Americans had never heard of Vietnam. In a few years it would be America's obsession. For John it was a new culture, a new life, and he was prepared to do God's will. This new country he was about to enter was filled with a people whose life was centered on the graven and contrived image of Buddha, the appeasing of evil spirits, or in many cases the harsh requirements of Roman Catholicism.

When he got off the plane at Tan Son Nhat Airport he was greeted by the usual heat and humidity common to Saigon on a daily basis. It was enough to knock a Northwesterner off his feet. But it served as a reality check that he really was on the foreign field to reap a harvest of souls and to do whatever he could to further the cause of Jesus Christ, the risen Savior. Being uncomfortable would be a small price to pay for securing for eternity the souls of the people of Vietnam.

John arrived in Vietnam alone. Josephine was a buyer at J. C. Penney in Spokane and would join him in a few months. But this was where he would stay. Bob Shelton was the field director in Vietnam for Overseas Crusades, and he greeted John and set him up at his duplex to study Vietnamese and speak from time to time to the Vietnamese military. John was to be an associate missionary and work with the Vietnamese nationals.

By the time John arrived in South Vietnam the political situation had turned for the worse. North Vietnam was governed by the Vietminh, led by Ho Chi Minh. Ho was an interesting mixture of Vietnamese nationalist and Marxist. The United States never considered having a close relationship with Ho because of his communist ties and his past with the Soviet Union. He had been trained by the Soviets early in his political career and, with the Cold War in full swing, was therefore not trusted by the United States government. The South was led by a noncommunist government set up by Vietnamese emperor Bao Dai, who was soon replaced by Ngo Dinh Diem, an autocratic tyrant who later fanned the antigovernment flames that would make American policy makers' lives very difficult.

The Geneva Accords had mandated that all of Vietnam hold elections to determine what kind of government would unite the country. South Vietnam, no doubt with U.S. advice, never let these elections take place. The government of North Vietnam and the communists of the south were determined to reunite the country. An armed effort was the only option for them. The country began another plunge into the horrors of a protracted war.

The United States gave immediate support to South Vietnam. The communists saw the U.S. as another foreign imperialist that needed to be ousted. This desire to unite and oust a foreign power was the primary motivation to fight. The communists had placed their hope in political liberation.

John and the many other missionaries who had come to Vietnam were indeed imperialists: they were going to spread the power and influence of Jesus as far as He would be accepted. Jesus could offer the only true liberation. Political liberation will always fall short of its expectations. Only Jesus could truly satisfy their innermost need. Only He could free them from the bondage and oppression of sin that has a grip on mankind much greater than any foreign power. John was there with the truth that sets people free. He was anxious to offer the message of true liberation.

Despite all the excitement of starting a new ministry, the honeymoon wore off quickly with the need to study the language. John studied Vietnamese for months, with little success. It is a difficult language, and even more difficult for someone in their forties who has never learned a foreign language before. John studied six to eight hours a day, making little progress. The process was a bit discouraging to a highly motivated man. It was the hardest work he had ever done in his life.

Overseas Crusades wanted him to be involved in a ministry with the Vietnamese military. He was preparing to set up meetings and evangelistic efforts at the huge military camps in the Saigon area as well as in the hospitals and prison camps that were being set up. The Vietcong (South Vietnamese communist guerrillas) were beginning their campaign of assassinating hundreds of village chieftains and launching a reign of terror and control over the countryside of South Vietnam. The numbers of injured and captured were growing. The short peaceful existence of South Vietnam was being shattered. They were frightful days for everyone. Danger was all around, and yet both John and Jo had an amazing courage and peace from God about coming to Vietnam. The insecurity of the days made an opportunity for the gospel, and John was to be the man to serve in this area.

One day he was asked by Bob Shelton to take a newspaper reporter and photographer representing World Vision up to the Central Highlands to see the work among the tribal people. John had been to that region several times in past visits to Vietnam. He took them to Jurin, a town about 70 kilometers from Da Lat (pronounced duh-lot), where missionaries Herb and Lydia Jackson of the Christian and Missionary Alliance worked. The Jacksons were working among the Koho (pronounced kuh-ha) speaking tribes, planting churches in the villages. They were opening a new Bible school that very night and had invited John and his guests to the ceremony. It was the result of years of work, and they were very excited to share the moment with others.

Before night fell Herb Jackson guided them on a tour of several churches from Jurin to Da Lat. It was an amazing testimony to the grace of God to see these churches already established. But there were thousands of mountain people still living a near-Stone Age existence, with a religion in which the entire goal was to try and satisfy unknown spirits with blood sacrifices so that good might come. The reporter and photographer got an eyeful in that one-day visit.

That night they attended the opening of the Jurin Bible School. It was a short walk to the longhouse where the school was being housed. The Koho longhouses are about 200 feet long and are raised up about 8 feet off the ground, and are made with a combination of bamboo, palm branches, and area pine. They typically house up to 120 people, with several families living in one house. Several fires would be going at the same time, spaced several feet apart down the length of the house. A constant haze of smoke hung in the air throughout the house, and it was filled with a host of aromas. At night the light was dim but adequate, once the eyes adjusted to it. To a Westerner it had an otherworldly appearance. As they approached the ladder to the longhouse John was struck by the aroma emanating from the building.

He had smelled this before in his previous visits to "tribesland," as John later called it, and he found it difficult to put into words what it smelled like. He now describes it as sort of a smoked ham smell. "It was the smell of the people," he recalls, a smell that was derived from time spent socializing and cooking around a fire in a smoke-filled house. To John, as he was struck with this "smell of the people" as he approached the house, it was as if it were the sweet aroma of Christ Himself.

As he moved toward the longhouse something amazing happened to John. He, at that moment, was flooded with a love for these people that he neither asked for nor sought. With each step he was flooded with more and more love and concern for these tribal people he had never met. With each step up the ladder tears began to fill his eyes, until by the time he reached the top and the entrance to the house he was weeping. It was as if each step represented a deeper level of affection for these strange people, and his awareness of their need for Christ deepened. He hadn't wept like this since the day he had received Christ back at that old tent meeting. He tried to hide his tears as he found his way to a spot to sit and watch the dedication service. No one seemed to be aware of John's emotions as he sat cross-legged in the dark shadows of the room. He wondered what it all meant. This was an extraordinary moment in his life. He knew that moment might change the very direction of his entire life. "Why now, and why here?" he thought.

Deep down he knew what this meant. He was home. This was another "calling" from the Lord, a more specific one this time. This is why the Lord had called him to Vietnam. Not to minister to the Vietnamese military. As good a ministry as that would be, he was here to work among the tribespeople. The "Montagnards," as the French called them. The full force of John's passion to serve Christ was poured out for these people he didn't even know yet. He felt a love for them

that only can be explained as the love of God. He understood the "agape" form of the word love more than any other
time in his life. He was at that moment willing to endure any
hardship, suffer any pain, perform any task in order for these
people to come to a saving knowledge of Jesus Christ. And
he would.

After the dedication ceremony for the Bible school he
escorted his guests back to their night's lodging. They were
unaware of John's personal experience in the longhouse.
The conversation centered on the work of the Jacksons and
how the church in the mountains was growing. John joined
in some of the conversation, but his mind was racing and
distracted, centered on the changes he would soon need
to make. He was going to have to get approval from the
mission to change his assignment. Since OC was not a tribal
mission organization this would be an unusual request. He
would also have to move to Da Lat and would need to begin
learning a new language other than Vietnamese. That didn't
sound so bad, since his Vietnamese wasn't going so well and
the climate of Da Lat was "Dalatful."

The next morning as they drove back to Saigon the
reporter, photographer, and John were relatively quiet, all
musing over their upcoming tasks. John was deep in thought
over the possibilities of working with the tribal people. His
lifetime desire was to preach the gospel where the name of
Christ had not been heard. It seemed he was at the point
where he might actually be able to do just that, the Lord
willing.

When he returned to Saigon he continued to study
Vietnamese, but the task was difficult for him, and his motivation was waning. He made precious slow progress, and
it was becoming discouraging. He was able to be involved
with gospel presentations, going to areas around Saigon
showing slides and films. It was a way for him to present the
message without having to know much of the language. He

was pleased to be serving the Lord, but he knew deep down inside that it was not his ministry to work primarily with the Vietnamese nationals.

In November 1958 John left for Hong Kong to meet Jo, who was coming to join him. That same month he approached Dick Hillis and Norm Cummings of Overseas Crusades about working among the mountain people of the Central Highlands. They felt it was likely to be a temporary thing. In fact, they felt that John's overseas missionary work was likely to be temporary. John would show them.

John would be the first to start a pioneering tribal work from their mission organization, and the mission wasn't sure if it wanted to go in that direction. However, after hearing of the call on John's life, as he explained what happened to him at the longhouse, they couldn't refuse to let him follow the Lord's leading. Soon John and Jo were making their way to Da Lat.

They got to Da Lat in time for the holidays. The Newmans immediately hired a cook and language teacher. John wasn't sure how this was going to work out, because language study in Saigon had been arduously slow. All he seemed to learn was how to do a little shopping in the street markets of Saigon. If Vietnamese was this hard, how could he ever learn a language that wasn't even written yet? But he soon found it was actually easier, and he made much better progress.

The six- to seven-hour-a-day sessions with his interpreter and language teacher, K'din (pronounced kuh-deen), were the hardest work he had ever done, and as many missionaries will tell you, language learning is some of the hardest work of being a missionary. The language he was to learn was called Koho. It was a versatile language in the Central Highlands, because you could communicate with several tribes to some degree.

John was not going to just sit around and learn words and phrases all day long, however. He wanted to tell these needy people about the love of Christ. He had other missionaries go with him each Sunday, and he would sing and give a message about Jesus to one of the tribal churches in the area. He managed to visit fifty-three different tribal churches by Christmas in his first year. All the visits were memorable, but all his communication had to be done through an interpreter, and he found it frustrating. This was exciting and he was being used of the Lord, but he wanted desperately to communicate with the people in their language. In many ways learning the Koho language was a humiliating process, and the progress seemed slow. But by the end of ten months he was able to deliver his first message in Koho.

It was a test of his competency. His audience was the large tribal church in Da Lat. He was to speak for ten minutes, and he had to be fluent enough that the majority would understand all that he said. He was as nervous as he had ever been in his life. Veteran missionaries came to hear the speech and serve as his evaluators. After his delivery they congratulated him for passing with flying colors. He was on his way now.

John ventured into the strategy of village-to-village evangelism. He knew his spiritual gift was evangelism, and because there were few nationals to do the work he felt the Lord was leading him to go out to the villages himself to preach the gospel. This is why it was so necessary to learn the native language. Fluency would help gain the respect of the people. A person who knew the language would much more likely be listened to than one who didn't. John learned each word with a sense of urgency. With the political situation of Vietnam so precarious, there was no telling how much time they would have left to share the word of salvation.

Going into a new village to preach was always exciting, because in some cases it was a people who had never heard the name of Jesus. But as always, the enemy was fierce. In many cases the power of evil spirits was evident. The primitive tribes of Southeast Asia were almost universally animists, ancestor worshippers, or demon worshippers. Though this was a big obstacle it also served sometimes as an advantage by showing the tribal people the contrast between their fallible faith and that of the living God.

Another obstacle for an outsider was earning the personal respect of the people. There needed to be a reason for coming to listen to a "white man." The messenger had to be someone they could trust and look up to in some way. John was able to establish a high level of esteem among the tribespeople through his hunting successes. Now, John was not exactly an experienced hunter, but he had some experience in the Pacific Northwest where he grew up, and he did enjoy hunting immensely. The Central Highlands were a hunter's paradise full of deer, tigers, leopard, and all sorts of fowl. Interestingly, the Lord was with John even in this venture.

Being a successful hunter was what impressed the "men among men" in this kind of society. It might compare to America's respect for professional athletes. John was able to show that he was a "mighty hunter." Once he shot an egret, a white bird about the size of a seagull, at 500 yards. Shot it right through the neck in the company of some tribal hunters. "It was a miracle," John said of the incident. "People may question the idea of shooting a bird at 500 yards for sport as a miracle, but it was." At that distance you had to lift your rifle several inches up to make allowance for the distance. "I had truly become the 'Great White Hunter' after that." This and many other such successes gave John the respect that was so necessary to be able to go to the various villages and preach, and more importantly, for them to listen.

As John's reputation preceded him in many cases, he was able to have the time of his life, sharing the gospel and hunting big game along the way. The mountain people were often protein starved. John's hunting was a source of food for the people he served, and they were very appreciative.

As John's hunting talents improved in the Central Highlands of Vietnam he often became a hunting guide for visitors to Da Lat.

When John recalls his hunting stories he quickly tells how he killed a 500-pound tiger. He knows that this is not very politically correct in these days, but he was proud of the accomplishment. Tigers were greatly feared among the mountain people and had been known to kill hundreds of people. A single tiger could kill scores of people.

John asked to be taken on a hunt. He was guided into the forests deep in the mountains and waited for a tiger to come down the road. He climbed up a tree and waited. It was late at night and there was little light, but soon a tiger appeared. The guides were down the road trying to coax a tiger out of the forest and lead it to John. They were completely unaware that John was about to confront the largest cat in the world all by himself. This tiger was one of the largest ever seen in the area. A shot rang out in the still night air, and the guides came running with fear. John took one shot and felled the beast in an instant. A failed shot could have injured it and enraged it to new heights of terror. The tribal guides came upon the scene not sure if John had silenced him or enraged him. To their relief they observed the lifeless frame of the tiger beneath the tree. John was still in the tree, and there was some commotion for a moment because they didn't know for sure it was dead. When the life refused to return to the tiger they drew closer to it, and John came down from the tree and soaked in the pleasure of his victory. Now that John had killed a potential threat to their people, with one shot, John was hailed by the tribesmen as a great hunter, and he enjoyed this status very much. John kept the huge pelt on the wall of his home in Da Lat.

The "Great White Hunter" found that this primitive people were very receptive to the gospel. When it came to sharing the greatest story ever told, the people were in many ways ripe for hearing. The people's religion had an elaborate system of sacrificing animals and spilling their blood to appease the anger of the spirits and bring about some good outcome. The Montagnards often sacrificed all their wealth in order to appease the spirits if they thought it was necessary. It was a heavy burden to the people. Killing a needed buffalo, pig, or chicken would take food and other means of support away from them just to make a spirit happy.

John would come along and tell them that God, the creator of all mankind, loved them so much that He gave His only Son as a blood sacrifice. This man, Jesus, walked the earth and experienced life as we have experienced life, but never disobeyed the Father. He alone lived up to the perfection that was required for full acceptance. He was hated by many and was sentenced to die by evil men. This was the plan of God the Father all along, so that His Son, Jesus, could be the perfect blood sacrifice for the sin of all humanity. He died even for the primitive tribes of the Central Highlands of Vietnam. When Jesus, His Son, was being killed God could have rescued Him, but He chose rather to place the sinful deeds of all humanity on Him. As Jesus hung on the cross he endured the harsh eternal punishment of all our sins, and God the Father's anger was appeased by this most perfect and complete sacrifice. No other sacrifice would be needed from that time on. Satan and his horde were defeated foes.

The people who heard about this Jesus and understood the good news with their hearts would say that the words were "delicious on my ears." What a perfect way to describe the gospel. John loved to tell how the gospel was delicious to the ears of his tribal brothers and sisters in Christ because it described better than any phrase how he felt when he received the gospel. It was indeed delicious to the ears among the tribal people. They would no longer have to sacrifice their chickens or water buffalo to appease the spirits. Jesus paid it all for them. John had the experience of leading many to the Savior in those early days through his village evangelism approach. He recalls a typical story of conversion which represented many such decisions.

One evening he ventured off into territory near a village he had never been before. He was certain they had never heard the name of Jesus. But this time he was going that way to hunt, not to evangelize. He wanted to shoot a gaur, or wild ox. He had heard that the meat was delicious and, of course, plentiful. A few of the village men he had been working with were with him on the hunt. As they were walking down the dirt road amongst the dense forest John spotted a large, dark beast that he was sure was a gaur. The shadows of the forest made the path dark. The beast's eyes gleamed, however, in the faint light that peeked through the trees and centered on it 200 meters away. The eyes were far apart, which fit the description of an ox, so John took a shot. Big mistake.

He hit the animal in the head, but it was right in the mouth, only wounding it. Soon some nearby tribesmen came out to see what had happened, and they discovered John had shot one of their water buffaloes. Besides the embarrassment, John now had a considerable public relations problem on his hands. The men from the village said it was the pet of one of the teenage girls in the village. Since he had only wounded it, he now had to finish the job right in front of his protesters. They demanded payment for the buffalo, and John agreed to pay 1,200 piasters, about 120 American dollars. But as usual, John saw this as an opportunity for sharing the gospel.

He said that he would pay the money, but they had to come to a large feast he would put on after they butchered the beast. They would be required to come and sit and listen to him give a service. The logic was twisted, but amazingly they agreed. John brought some of his friends with him a few days later, and the whole village enjoyed the buffalo together and sat and listened to John share the good news about Jesus and His sacrifice for them. Five men, some young and some old, prayed to receive Christ into their hearts that night.

Like so many other villages he evangelized he went back to this group on a regular basis, and each time more and more came to the Savior. As time went on, a small, short-term Bible school was set up at the village. The thrill of leading a people who had never heard the name of Jesus spoken before was indescribable. And it happened time and again. God was building His church, and John was excited to be a part of that process, to be one of the work crew.

That wasn't the end of the story, however. The night of the feast, a "diinsa" (pronounced dee-in-say), or village representative to the government of South Vietnam, was present. He didn't receive Christ that night, and he seemed quite uninterested in the message. However, not much later he was at another service in another village. John noticed him, and Sao A and a few other Christian men from the church sat down to talk with him and share more clearly the plan of eternal life. They tried very hard to convince this man to pray. He had a peculiar reaction, however.

The men could not understand why he would not convert, because he seemed very interested by this time, but he would not make that simple step of faith. They talked some more, but the man could not speak. He seemed disturbed and frustrated. As soon as the men asked him to pray the "sinner's prayer" he was forced to stop. The men talked and talked some more, thinking he just needed more convincing.

They soon found out that he literally could not speak the name of "Jesus." As soon as he tried, he would balk. They sensed the Holy Spirit was speaking to the heart of this man, so the men prayed more. It is presumed that the very power of demons was preventing him from saying the only name under heaven by which men can be saved. There was a major battle going on for this soul. After more prayer on the part of the church leaders, and out of his genuine desire to come to the Savior, the man was finally able to muster the strength to whisper the name of "Jesus." At that moment he was set free and he knew it. It wasn't any loud or dramatic moment, but the man was born again into God's kingdom.

The diinsa's conversion was definitely real. He grew steadily in the knowledge of the Lord and became a leader among the tribal churches. John sees in this story something that represented much of his ministry in Vietnam. He witnessed how the good news of God, the Creator, providing the only complete sacrifice for sins once for all through Jesus Christ, was difficult to resist when understood in the heart. These people could be set free from the burdensome belief system of sacrifices that they had been practicing for centuries. The Spirit of God spoke to the heart of this man and then drew him to Himself. John also saw the power of Satan as an ever-present enemy to the gospel, but at the name of Jesus the people could be saved. That gospel was indeed "the power of God for salvation to everyone who believes, to the Jew first and ..." also to the small mountain tribes of Vietnam (Rom 1:16).

Chapter 5

The Army in White

The United States had been supporting the government of South Vietnam since Vietnam had been divided after the French left in 1954. The communist North posed a significant and symbolic threat to U.S. interests in Southeast Asia. With the Cold War going full steam, American policymakers thought it would be a devastating blow to lose one more country to the communists. In the late fifties, Eisenhower decided that the U.S. should provide military advisors and military equipment to the South. In an effort to reunify Vietnam under one communist regime, the communists stepped up their pressure on the South with a campaign of terror. They assassinated village chieftains and government officials throughout the country and left their bodies in full view of the community. Over 60,000 South Vietnamese officials were killed this way over a two-year period. The atmosphere of the country was one of constant crisis and terror. These were the conditions that John and Jo Newman came to in their missionary service.

When John F. Kennedy assumed the presidency in 1961 he found that policy in Asia was potentially a political nightmare, but he was resolved to step up assistance to the needy South Vietnamese as they faced increasing pressure from the

North. In the early part of the war, Vietnam was rarely in the news; on occasion, a casualty was reported. Kennedy's credibility as a cold warrior was on the line, and he was not about to appear too soft on communism. He did, however, begin to show signs of doubt later in his term. By 1963 he had authorized sending 16,000 advisors to Vietnam to meet the threat of a communist takeover. The U.S. Army Special Forces (Green Berets) were the heart of Kennedy's effort to help South Vietnam.

In that same year there is evidence that the CIA helped orchestrate the coup that overthrew President Diem. The U.S. perceived that Diem's autocratic approach to governing could cost them the country. The Buddhists were also protesting his policies, and the world witnessed a Buddhist priest set himself on fire in the streets of Saigon on the front pages of their newspapers and evening news. They were turbulent days, and something had to be done.

It was believed that the significant increase in U.S. support would deter the North from continuing its campaign. It seemed to do the opposite. After the assassination of President Kennedy in November 1963, President Lyndon Johnson seemed determined to take a more aggressive role in Vietnam.

The significance of stepping up the United States commitment to Vietnam was that it might lead to better protection for the missionaries and allow the work of the gospel to go on for many more years. At the same time, the communist forces were stepping up their efforts, and the threat of South Vietnam falling was all too real by 1964.

So John and Jo found themselves serving Christ in what was one of the most threatening places on earth at the time. It took the love of Jesus to be willing to risk all for the cause of helping to save some. The task of serving seemed overwhelming. John saw so many needs before him every day. People's most basic needs were often going unfulfilled all around him. The absence of food, shelter, clothing, and medical attention was a constant threat.

As in any endeavor, strategy is important. Success is often dependent on a well-thought-out and logical plan of action. John's strategy to spread the Word was not limited to some seminary textbook. He had full freedom to spread the gospel any way he saw best. He was able to be led by the Holy Spirit and apply basic common sense and nothing else. It was an exciting time. In the midst of war he felt safe, because he knew he was in the center of God's will.

However, being in such a dangerous country gave a heightened sense of urgency to get the work of the ministry done. As has been mentioned before, the Lord quickly led John in the direction of village evangelism. He took this method from Dr. Dick Hillis, the founder of his mission organization, Overseas Crusades.

Dick Hillis worked among the Chinese people before China's fall to communism in 1949. Instead of the traditional method of going into a region and establishing a Bible school as a training center and working to train pastors for churches, Hillis would select a young man from one of the villages who showed signs of being a preacher and would take him along as he traveled to other villages. The young preacher would be given a chance to preach and study. It seemed to be a great way to accomplish two goals at the same time: evangelize and train. John saw that the same kind of door was open to him in the Central Highlands of Vietnam. Through his village evangelism he would likewise bring along a young, faithful man to share in the preaching and evangelizing work. The Lord blessed this method richly.

The typical village visit would require a journey of several hours, or in some cases, days. He would set up a time for the meeting, usually at night. The people would know in advance that John and his evangelistic team of tribal folks would be there. He would show Bible slides and preach, or simply preach. There would always be lots of singing. The tribal people loved to sing. The meetings would be held out in the open air, or if a church existed, they would meet in the church. John would make several village visits a week.

It was a wonderful time for John to get to know the various pastors in the region and share the gospel whenever he had the opportunity. As he found out, sharing the gospel was actually pretty easy in tribal land. These primitive people didn't have all the complex philosophical and polit-ical barriers that so many people have in modern times. They were simple people. Often all they required was to point out to them creation and speak of the Great Creator and explain the ultimate blood sacrifice of Jesus, the Son of the Creator, and they would understand. After the message they would be asked to "don mo jat" (believe and follow). The wonderful thing about John's village evangelism ministry is that they would often *don mo jat.*

The "believe and follow" message could sometimes be a problem. On occasion, John and the other mission-aries and tribal pastors would be misunderstood. The tribal people would think they were to follow Mr. Jackson, Mr. Tot (a Vietnamese missionary to the tribal people), or Mr. Newman. But they would soon be corrected and led to the One who is to be followed.

Not every outing was a success, however. Out of the stubbornness of their hearts, many would reject the message in order to continue in their old ways. And on occasion there would even be some humorous responses. John remembers in particular the "belching man."

Many of the tribal folks would come to the services out of curiosity and/or boredom. It was not unusual for John to see new faces in the crowd. One night when John was preaching, as he was developing his message to its proper climax, all of a sudden something broke the flow of his words. In the middle of the most important part of John's message a man sitting right in the front row stretched his arms and yawned loudly, and then let out a loud, long belch. It sort of startled John and stopped him mid-sentence, and he chuckled to himself. The man had been drinking and was looking for a little entertainment. Apparently John wasn't quite giving him what he needed. A little humility was good once in a while, John thought.

There was no such thing as an average day for the Newmans. They had to take care of many day-to-day affairs just like anyone else, but often it entailed much more. There was always some new need. But John's passion was to go to the villages. His dream was to reach as many as he could. To preach the name of Jesus where the name of Jesus hadn't been heard before was also his dream, and it was fulfilled many times over.

One such time came when he went to two unreached villages whose inhabitants were known as the Red-Tasseled Ma people because they wore a distinguishing red scarf around their heads. To get to these villages John had to drive his British-made Land Rover to the regions beyond Da Lat and cross the Krong Kno River multiple times. His evangelistic team went as far as they could on the road, and then from there they were to use horses to get to these villages. Horse travel was very common for John during his time in Vietnam. The horses were very small—so small that an average-sized American adult's legs would almost touch the ground as they rode—but they were strong and able to handle the steep green mountains of the Central Highlands.

After they drove to the furthest village by road, they got there to find out that the horses they were going to ride were sick. In the village where they were to pick up the horses the tribal folks wanted to go for a ride in John's Land Rover. Such entertainment couldn't be passed up, they thought. So John took them on a little ride through the village. The typical village had a lane separating two rows of longhouses, about 200 yards in length. As he neared the end of the village a man carrying a lamp in the back of the Land Rover jumped out. John hadn't noticed him get out and began to back up the Land Rover because the lane was so narrow. The old man didn't notice John backing up and was hit by the vehicle, and the lamp he was carrying fell and was broken.

The man wasn't hurt, but the lamp was extremely important to the trip because the services were in the evening and the lamp gave the people light. The light of the gospel would not be dimmed, however. With the lamp out and the horses sick, John was still determined to reach these tribes. He decided to walk to their villages in spite of not having the horses. This meant climbing up and down steep mountains on narrow trails. It was much more exhausting than using the horses, but the burden was light because he knew that he would be delivering the most important news they could possibly ever hear.

When he got to the villages of the Red-Tasseled Ma people he was able to get the people to build fires for lighting because the lamp had been broken. They weren't sure it would be enough light, but it turned out to be enough. It was never known how the people might respond to the message of salvation. With a few of the details not going exactly right, John was a bit nervous at first. The Lord soon reminded him that it was He who would cause the increase. All they were to do was plant and water. That wonderful night, the light of His Word exposed the need for a personal Savior to seven people, and they prayed to receive Christ. John was able to leave with them a young preacher to work with them for a while and explain further the things of God.

As they traveled to the next village of Red-Tasseled Ma people John's team rejoiced in what tremendous grace the Lord had shown. The gospel is truly the power of God for salvation to everyone who believes. At the next village they again relied on the light of fires, and more so on the light of the gospel. Five people came to a saving knowledge of Christ. John was able to send a young preacher to that village as well a few days later. What an exciting time.

John's responsibility began to expand as he came to know and love the people of the mountains. He soon realized that he couldn't just go around and share the gospel with these people and not be concerned for their physical needs. Their needs were great at times. The Vietcong's strategy in the war was to control the countryside as much as possible among the Vietnamese people. The tribal people were not always their concern, but as the war grew from year to year the mountain people were being affected by the war.

As the war came closer, John took an increasing role in helping supply their needs. As time went on his ministry actually evolved into a type of social work. Over time he served as a distributor of food and housing materials, organized relocation efforts, and administered a language school, medical clinic, and nutrition clinic. John did it all. He was never trained to do any of this kind of work, yet he did it. He did it for two reasons: one, because there was nobody else to do the needed work, and two, because he claimed the promise in Philippians 4:13, "I can do all things through Him who strengthens me." Much of John's life has been this way. The power of the indwelling Holy Spirit gave him the courage to tackle every challenge that lay before him.

John found himself often unloading trucks full of bulgur wheat that he had secured for the people. John would coordinate pickup and delivery of this food. Interestingly, the nationals were often bothered by seeing John actually do physical work. They saw missionaries as professional people and thought they should hire out these kinds of duties. It wasn't uncommon for missionaries to hire grounds-keepers and cooks just to provide some employment to the nationals.

When one lives in the secure borders of the United States or Canada death is common, but untimely death is more the exception than the rule. Catastrophes happen, but they are few, and the cost in lives is usually lessened by modern technology or medicine. In Vietnam, a primitive country by our standards and in the middle of a war, death was as common as the setting sun. John and Jo's hearts were often wrenched by the death of people they worked with. They could not prepare themselves for this part of missionary work, but it came with the territory, even more so in the land of Vietnam where they chose to serve. They often found that God supplied them with the grace to go on even when their hearts were broken.

The dangers in Vietnam came not only from war, but from nature as well. The tropical climate brought a season of monsoon rains and typhoons. The delicate balance of life could be upset by anything unusual. One such occurrence happened in 1964.

The catastrophe hit Vietnam right in the middle of an escalation phase of the war. The rainy season had come, but this time with a vengeance. It was the worst flooding the country had seen in decades. In the late summer and early fall, three typhoons hit, one right after the other. The typhoons' greatest strength hit the Philippines, but the rain hit Vietnam. It rained for twenty days and twenty nights. One half of Noah's experience, and it seemed like it in Vietnam, John recalls.

The number killed by the flooding was estimated at 11,000 people. As in any land, the people live close to their water source. The rivers rapidly swelled to levels unimaginable to the people. Not only did the rivers swell, but the typhoons caused the tides to rise, and tidal waves were crashing in from the ocean as well.

People lined the riverbanks, hoping to launch a boat, but they couldn't and many were swept away by the tidal waves. Bodies could be seen everywhere. Livestock was lost in incredible numbers. The situation was desperate for the survivors, who often were stranded on newly made islands with the waters rising.

John immediately mobilized efforts to bring assistance to the flood-weary people. He used his contacts in America to quickly raise money to assist in the relief effort. One of his first contacts was his faithful friend Merv Rosell. Merv sent $1,000 immediately to help pastors in the flood-affected area. The pastors would use some for themselves, because they were always deeply affected by this kind of crisis. The pastors would also use some of the money for rebuilding their churches.

John's keen sense of the importance of communicating the need for money wherever the gospel is concerned came into full expression. It was one of his fortes before he was a missionary in Vietnam, and it was definitely useful now. So he secured a plane to take himself and a few other missionaries for an aerial tour of the flood-affected areas to take pictures. The pictures would be important to share in America the desperate need of thousands of Vietnamese people. John had developed a special relationship with the military, and they would often take him to places he needed to go. It could also be dangerous; on this trip the Vietcong fired on the plane that John was on. The Vietcong continued their relentless attacks even in the midst of this natural catastrophe.

One pastor had tried to rebuild his destroyed church shortly after the first typhoon. But the entire rebuilding job was destroyed by the second typhoon. It was a discouraging time for the people of the Central Highlands. It was estimated that 95 percent of their crops had been destroyed and 93 percent of their livestock had drowned. As John flew over the ravaged terrain, those estimates sounded conservative to him.

It was a horrible sight to see firsthand all the death and destruction. From the plane you could see the floating bodies being swept away and hundreds of bloated livestock. There was nothing but water where villages and cropland once existed as far as you could see. It was hard to imagine the region would ever be the same.

Through the efforts of John and others, thousands of dollars were sent to help the people of Vietnam during these difficult days. It was a testimony to the love of Jesus and His people around the world. Providing assistance to anyone who might need it was a way to share the love of Christ. John and the other missionaries he worked with knew this all too well. To preach the love and forgiveness of Christ in the midst of this suffering and not help their physical needs would be insulting. They had to do anything they could to help these people, and they did. John received much satisfaction from this kind of work. In essence it was social work, but in reality it was spiritual work.

Amazingly, God showed particular mercy upon believers in this flood. Of the 11,000 people killed in this flood, it was reported that only a few of the 11,000 were Christians. The Vietnamese and mountain people didn't see this as some odd coincidence. They recognized the special hand of God on their behalf and rejoiced in His love.

God's special protection can be illustrated in one account told by John. In one area a village had been completely destroyed. The homes were flattened and submerged in water. The entire area had changed color. The once-vibrant greens had turned to a sea of brown. One Christian family had managed in the midst of the storm and subsequent rushing water to climb up on their roof. The rushing floodwaters had made their roof a temporary but unstable island. They were found clinging to their roof and had been there for days. The South Vietnamese army was sent up to the Central Highlands to help in the relief. They came upon the stranded family, and the soldiers were reluctant to help them, out of fear for their own lives. One officer forced the soldiers under his command at gunpoint to go after this family. They were eventually rescued and gave praise to God.

As help came in to the many Christian workers in the region, the unbelieving population began to notice. They saw how God seemed to protect so many professing Christians. This laid the groundwork for many Vietnamese to respond to the gospel in the months and years to come. God was showing the people of this long, narrow strip of land in Southeast Asia that He loved them and that it was in their best interest both now and for eternity to pay attention to His message.

Even as a natural catastrophe was hitting the country of Vietnam the war intensified greatly. This made conditions for the people of South Vietnam even more difficult. The year 1964 was a pivotal time for the war. In August of that year the North Vietnamese fired on the U.S. destroyers Turner Joy and Maddox while they were off the coast of North Vietnam in the Gulf of Tonkin. This event is now shrouded in controversy as to what really happened and why, but it set a course of action for the United States that wouldn't be changed for many years to come.

President Johnson was deeply concerned about the possible fall of South Vietnam to the communists and their new boldness in challenging the U.S. presence in the area. He asked Congress for the authority to repel aggression in Southeast Asia in the Gulf of Tonkin Resolution. He got this approval with only two dissenting votes from both houses of Congress combined. He quickly sent new troops to Vietnam and ordered retaliatory bombing raids over North Vietnam. Since the coup that overthrew Diem the people of South Vietnam had not been satisfied with the replacement government, so students and Buddhists again demonstrated in the streets. At the same time, Johnson was running for election.

This also began the ever-careful and unsuccessful attempt to fight the war without stepping on too many political toes.

John was not without his opinion on American politics of the time, for politics had a tremendous effect on how his ministry would go in Vietnam. Decisions in Washington would have a direct impact upon the very people with whom he worked.

One of the strategies that was developed for Vietnam was the "strategic hamlet" program. Under this program, the government would fortify key villages throughout the country. In one such village an amazing work of God took place.

Shortly after the flood, John headed to Phuoc Luong to visit the strategic hamlet there. He came to visit and size up the situation with the four pastors of the churches there. They told him a story that still thrills his heart.

The village was located near the Krong Kno River Valley. The strategic hamlet was made up of three language groups and about four tribes, including the Rade, Roglai, and Tring people. They originated high up in the mountains of the Central Highlands but moved closer to the ocean in order to escape from the Vietcong. The VC attacked constantly and burned down their churches. With the VC in pursuit they had to take their belongings and load them on precarious rafts and float themselves down the river. They would have suffered great loss of life if they hadn't left when they did. The escape was a miracle in itself.

When they arrived in Phuoc Luong they were at the mercy of the government to help them relocate. They set up a village of about 1,300 people, with four Christian churches among them. This was an unusual village, because they built a bamboo fence around the entire perimeter.

The mountain people were always on the side of the Americans. This made them targets for attack by the VC. The village actually had two fences of crisscrossed bamboo shoots sticking ten to fifteen feet in the air. The fences were about twenty feet apart, encircling the entire village, with sharpened bamboo shoots about four feet high sticking up in between, making two formidable barriers for any intruder.

In spite of the fortified "moat" type of structure to protect the people, they were far from safe. The village was set out in the open, surrounded by rice fields and patchy forests. In the daytime the mountain people would tend the rice field or forage for firewood to sell to the local Vietnamese. They were extremely poor, but were amazingly of great cheer because of their love for the Lord. Though not all villagers were Christians, most were in this village, and they dominated village life.

The government gave them just two small-caliber rifles and supplied two guards for the entire hamlet. The VC began their attack against the village. At first it was not that intense, but still very unnerving with just two rifles to protect all the people. It was the practice of the mountain churches to meet every night for a message and prayer. The prayers of these people would inspire the faith of a prodigal. The deep sincerity of their faith was electric. These prayer times intensified and lengthened as the VC began to step up their attacks on the new village. The VC were apparently getting hungry from the loss of food due to the recent flooding. They were coming down out of the mountains where they often hid from government forces. They decided to control the tribal villages so they wouldn't starve.

Amazingly, the small guard was able to hold off the superior VC force. As they endured increasing attacks they appealed to the government for more weapons and guards. They were able to get a total of fifty guns and fifty guards. This helped, but not nearly as much as the nightly prayers of the mountain people meeting in the four churches inside the hamlet. They prayed, and they sang hymns. They sang at the top of their lungs, right in the middle of being attacked. In one case they sang and prayed all night long. In spite of how late they stayed up, in the morning they would carefully go out into their fields and work on the crops or forage for more wood. This was very dangerous, because they had to venture outside of the protected area.

The VC had killed four people during this extended assault. All of those casualties happened outside the village. In all practicality, the VC should easily have been able to take the village. But they were prevented every time they tried. As the fight went on, word was making its way back that the Vietcong were certain they could take the village if it weren't for the "army in white," as they called it. The army in white would scare them off, and they would shrink back into the woods.

Who was this army in white that the VC were seeing? Was it the figment of their collective imagination? A result of drugs? Certainly the atheistic Vietcong would not know. They would assume some natural cause. However, once the village people heard this story they knew what it meant. There was only one reasonable explanation for what was being reported: the Lord was protecting them with His mighty angels. The prayers of a simple people were calling down the very protection of heaven for them, the kind of protection that comes rarely in human history. The kind of protection Elisha the prophet had.

Pastor Karr, a tribal pastor, remembers praying one night during the siege of the strategic hamlet near Phuoc Luong on a high hill along with his wife. As they were praying, a bright light filled their house in an amazing moment of glory. There was no rational explanation for the origin of this light. It filled him with awe. It was an assurance that he didn't need, but it was an amazing gift from the Lord for him and his wife, who were giving their lives for the gospel to the desperate people of Vietnam.

He recalled seeing that same light emanating from the hamlet under siege. He could see it from a distance one night as mortar shells and gunfire broke the silence of the cool mountain air. He thought at first it was a fire in the village, but found out later there was no such fire. He didn't know what it was, because he knew that the villagers could not create that much light. He wasn't at all surprised at the reports of the "army in white." It was the only thing that made sense. It was their Savior's heavenly servants out of His rich mercy protecting them.

John was also in awe as he heard this story firsthand from the pastors of the four churches. He rejoiced with them and marveled at God's evident love for these mountain people. In the midst of these floods and attacks he was able to give them food and other supplies from the $1,000 gift provided by Merv Rosell. Life was never so full and eternity never so real.

Chapter 6

He Who Is Greatest among You Shall Be Servant of All

J ohn loved village evangelism. It was the fulfillment of his ultimate dream. To be amidst the people for whom God had given him such love thrilled him each time he journeyed to see them in the mountains. The chance to share the saving knowledge of Jesus Christ with a village chief or make the first contact with a remote tribe was the ultimate experience for a missionary. John and Jo were having the time of their lives.

In their minds it was no sacrifice to leave the comforts of America. Their missionary term was an adventure. In fact, every trip to the villages was an adventure, in many ways not unlike a safari or exotic hunting trip. John's method of operation usually involved a five- or six-day trip. He would gather his team, comprised of some young people to sing and give testimony, and perhaps a village pastor. They would gather provisions and set off for a village tour. Sometimes the trip entailed traveling down a river in a dugout boat or trekking over the mountains on horseback. In some cases they traveled by foot, but that was avoided if at all possible. No location was easy to get to, but the journey itself was a lesson in the kingdom of God, the pearl of great price or the field of great value. Placing high priority on the spiritual well-being of these people of the mountains was as natural to John as breathing the fresh mountain air.

He loved the traveling experiences that the village visits afforded. Gliding down a river in a dugout, watching the beautiful greenery, was breathtaking. The wild animals that would surprise them on occasion made things exciting. The wonderful birds, the noise of the monkeys, and the challenge of each mountain made each trip a reminder of how blessed he was to be there. It was the closest thing to paradise he could imagine, and he got to live there every day.

Paradise aside, this was also a land of war and spiritual darkness. The job of sharing the light of God's Word was awesome and urgent. There was no telling how much more time would be allowed to work among these people. That fact and the inner drive to share the love of Christ could lead almost anyone to exhaustion.

Going up and down 1,000-foot elevations from one village to the other could wear a person out. And it did. As the years went by the thrill never ceased, but the body and soul needed some refreshment every once in a while.

In order for the missionaries and Vietnamese and tribal pastors to get some spiritual refreshment from time to time they would hold pastors conferences. John was often involved with their planning. One memorable conference took place in Da Lat in February 1966. Merv Rosell sent $500 just for the conference and its expenses. Norm Nelson, an accomplished American tenor soloist, came to refresh the men with his singing, and several missionaries preached.

The conference hall was jammed to capacity. Vietnamese pastors, missionaries, and tribal pastors came from all over the war-torn country. For most of them, coming to Da Lat was a vacation in itself because of its temperate climate. Its location almost 5,000 feet above sea level in the tropics made it one of the most comfortable places on earth. The majority of the folks attending lived with the sweltering, humid heat of the lowlands. The Da Lat pastors conference was as refreshing to their bodies as it was to their souls.

Their souls were renewed with the encouraging words of Glenn Johnson, the songs of Norm Nelson, and the stories of Herb Jackson. They all shared their experiences of triumph and struggle as the war and Satan made the spreading of the gospel difficult. One by one they exhorted and encouraged one another. The momentum of the conference seemed to build with each contribution. As the conference concluded with a strong, reverberating crescendo they sensed a deeper renewal than they had even hoped for. They prayed together and found a oneness that brought each of them great joy.

At the end of the conference Pastor Karr shared a testimony. This was no ordinary testimony, however. He stood up slowly to approach the podium. He seemed excessively humble, almost as if he were ill and barely had the strength to speak. But he began speaking in low, slow tones. He started off by saying he needed to confess that his heart had grown cold over the past few months. Due to the escalation of the war a crippling fear had come over him, and it had caused him to lose his love for ministry. His love for people had also grown lukewarm. He struggled with this in his soul, often denying that he was feeling this way. He had kept this to himself for months. He had kept ministering, but the passion had grown cold. As he was sitting in the conference listening to all the talks, songs, and testimonies, the Lord was quietly warming his heart once again. As he stood at the end of the conference to share how the Lord had warmed his heart in a special way and that he now had a renewed passion for His work, he was inspiring the other men. There wasn't a dry eye in the place after he spoke. It was the icing on the cake for this conference. These men were fired up to go on with the vital ministry God had given them. These pastors conferences were used by God to refresh those serving in Vietnam throughout the war.

After the Gulf of Tonkin incident and the passage of the Gulf of Tonkin Resolution, America took charge of most war operations. U.S. bombing missions began in earnest, and the number of troops began to grow to what eventually would be about 550,000 by 1969.

The missionaries looked on this policy change largely with favor, because it meant more protection for them and the people. However, as time went on some changed their view, seeing that the communists matched each escalation phase with their own.

As the war came closer and closer to the mountain people of the Central Highlands the village-to-village evangelism became more complicated. The needs of the people grew with each passing month. Taking a neutral position on the war was impossible. The tribal people were harassed by the Vietcong and North Vietnamese, who stole their food, took their land, or forced them to become a base of operations. The Vietnamese nationals (communist or not) were antagonistic to the tribal people already, and with the war they were subject to all kinds of cruelty. For years the war centered mostly in the lowlands, but it was moving toward the mountains and the Central Highlands. The tribes were primitive relative to their counterparts, the Vietnamese, and they were being thrust into a twentieth-century political and philosophical battle that they didn't understand or care to be a part of. However, they had no choice; it was coming to them.

All the people wanted to do was to be left alone to grow their crops and develop their land. The war wouldn't allow them that luxury, and the mountain people began to suffer. As John saw the needs grow he was reminded of James 2:14-17: "What use is it, my brethren, if someone says he has faith, but he has no works? ... If a brother or sister is without clothing and in need of daily food, and one of you says to them, 'Go in peace, be warmed and be filled,' and yet you do not give them what is necessary for their body, what use is that? Even so faith, if it has no works, is dead, being by itself." John knew that he had to do more and more to meet their physical needs. The early days of going from village to village having service after service had to be backed up with efforts to feed the people, cure their diseases, and find them shelter when they were displaced. John loved being able to make a difference. He rose to the occasion and became a one-man relief organization for the tribal people of Vietnam by coordinating other relief organizations' resources to assist the tribal people. In the process he saved hundreds of lives.

One of the first ministries that John had outside of his normal village work was assuming the directorship of the language school in Da Lat which served to teach Americans and other non-national people in Vietnam the Vietnamese language. The school struggled in the early years and even closed down for a year.

Under John's direction the language school developed into a more stable operation. It was fully equipped with the best Tanberg tape recording system for individualized student instruction. The school was useful to almost all the missionary efforts in Vietnam, from the Southern Baptists to the Roman Catholics. It developed the reputation for being the best language school in Southeast Asia. John was very proud of this accomplishment.

This was one of the first administrative responsibilities in his life. He was not a trained administrator or educator, but here he was director of the Da Lat Language School. He asked the Lord to give him the courage and strength to do the job he had been temporarily called to do. As John would see, the Lord answered this prayer and would also answer similar prayers that would be taking place in the future. God was using the language school experience to train John for other administrative duties. John just didn't know it at the time.

John found it took a special kind of vision to see the need to attend to details in the business of relief and school. He was a big-picture kind of guy and tried to leave the details to someone else. But now that he was the director of a school he had to take care of such details as the upkeep of the machines, reports, payroll, finances, the needs of the students, and those of the teachers. Though it took time away from his village work, he was comforted in the knowledge that the school was equipping many to do the work of the gospel more effectively.

Merv Rosell, the man John had met just before boarding the plane to Vietnam as a missionary, became a major source for raising funds for the needy people of the Central Highlands. Merv's evangelistic organization contributed thousands of dollars over the years. John would simply send a message to Merv about the needs, and the money would be there in days. Often Merv would send money before a need had arisen, and it would be near the exact amount for the next pressing need. John often marveled at how God worked these things out.

John's relief work was used by the Lord to be a living testimony of His grace. It was oftentimes simply miraculous the way the Lord's timing worked in the supplying of their needs. John, who was serving as the chief cook and bottle washer in these relief efforts, was often placed in a position where he had to make very quick and potentially life-saving decisions on how to spend the money. In spite of the great burden this was to him, he still enjoyed being used of the Lord.

John also worked with mission organizations other than Overseas Crusades. He was the first director of relief for World Vision in Vietnam. This required that he make periodic trips to Saigon for banking and collection of supplies. One time World Vision gave the Koho people a tractor. In the interests of seeing that the mountain people succeed in their agricultural work, World Vision thought this would be a useful gift. John became, by default, responsible for the tractor, something he later wished he hadn't become.

First of all, maintaining a tractor involved mechanical knowledge, something that was not exactly in the tribal people's repertoire. Not really in John's, either. So a man from the village was appointed to take care of the village tractor. The village had a big ceremony dedicating the tractor and thanking the Lord Jesus for His provision. Not many days after the dedication, the curator of the tractor was learning to maneuver the big machine and ran right over a bamboo shoot, puncturing a tire.

This was no small problem. The tire for the tractor cost $1,600 to replace. That's $1,600 in 1960s money. The blessing had become a burden. The tractor, just days in use, was all of a sudden useless. The man who popped the tire was humiliated and felt terrible. Getting the repair money would be no easy task, and getting the tire up to the tribal land would be just as difficult. The Lord was gracious, and in time through the generous donations of Americans the tribal folks got their tractor back, using it with a great deal more caution this time.

As John's leadership abilities became more and more apparent he was given more responsibilities. He had access to funds from the Mennonite Central Committee, the National Association of Evangelicals, World Relief Fund, Food for the Hungry, and of course Merv Rosell's Global Concern fund. Many times he could even enlist the support of the U.S. government to help with the emergency needs of the people.

As time went on, more mountain people, and even the people already living in the valleys, were forced to move to towns with a greater military presence. John remembers relocating 1,500 villagers to Da Lat from the Dran Valley. The U.S. Agency for International Development (USAID) gave some assistance by providing metal roofing. John was ultimately the man in charge because of his command of the language and his ability to work with the tribal people. In order to carry out this task he had to coordinate working with the U.S. military, South Vietnamese intelligence, and the government of South Vietnam.

Relocation first involved educating the people as to what they were going to do, trying to alleviate their fears and stress as much as possible. Then there was the task of forcing an entire village community to leave their homes. They had to organize putting everything they owned on their backs or in a cart to make the journey. The sight was a familiar one throughout the war: a long train of people loaded with their goods, headed down a narrow dirt road. It was heartbreaking. Yet John was always a pillar of strength for the people, along with Pastor Sau A and other village Christian leaders.

The tragedies of war were all around. The U.S. bombing of North Vietnam during the phase known as Operation Rolling Thunder gave the hope that the North would give up the fight. It seemed to do the opposite. The VC began to be bolder in their attacks, and the tribal casualties were mounting. The U.S. found that the Montagnards were very helpful and trained some to help in the war effort. This was helpful for the Americans, but it began to set the North Vietnamese Army (NVA) and the VC against the mountain people.

War has enough of its own tragedies, but when other natural disasters such as flooding, drought, and disease happen in the midst of war, resources are often not available to meet the needs of suffering people. John recalls that while in the midst of a corn and rice crop failure among the Roglai Tribe near Tong Luong a careless, drunken tribesman was carrying a torch one night and set nine thatched houses ablaze. Immediately ten families were made homeless. They were already hungry, without money to replace their homes or buy food. Amazingly, Merv Rosell sent John an unexpected sum of money, so he was able to apply it to the needs of the Roglai people.

In 1966 the war was coming closer to the Central Highlands all the time. One hundred VC snuck into the Kiam Li Airport one night and destroyed a helicopter, an I-19 observation plane, and the communications hut, and shot up a few planes. Two South Vietnamese soldiers were killed in the attack. This was the first attack made on Da Lat proper in the whole war. It was a sign that things were changing.

By 1967 more and more villages were being displaced due to attacks in the mountains. John was finding it difficult to keep up with the demands. One of the demands was to find housing materials. He was able to purchase aluminum roofing for the newly displaced villages. He found out that the tin roofing they had been using was inferior. It rusted rapidly in the hot, humid climate and was quickly useless. The aluminum was rustproof and much cooler for the residents.

With the financial resources available to John he was able to secure all kinds of supplies—a hundred bags of rice here, a hundred pounds of wheat there, aluminum roofing, 12,000 piasters to help some pastors. Whatever the need, John was finding out how he could help, because he could help. It was a heavy responsibility, but for the most part it humbled him. He asked God for wisdom, then did whatever made sense and was prudent, and God received the glory.

The big needs were not absent of individual heartache and suffering. Sau A was traveling through a small village when a handful of villagers ran up to him in desperation with a sick child. The four-year-old child had swallowed some poison. They didn't know what to do, and they didn't have the confidence in their sacrifices to have any success. They turned to Sau A.

Sau immediately rushed the child to the hospital in the Dran Valley. They never made it. The child died on the way. The sadness was deep. The mother and father and grandmother cried their eyes out. Though death was not uncommon in Vietnam or for the mountain people, it touched Sau in a special way. It broke his heart. He realized the depth of the love one has for a child and how so many of his countrymen were without hope in the world. This one situation gave Sau a renewed sense of urgency. He knew that they could have hope for eternal life even in the midst of their war-torn, tragic country.

Ha Jimmy and Ha Johnny were becoming John's right-hand men. They were the sons of Sau A (whose story is told in *The Bamboo Cross* by Homer Dowdy). Jimmy and Johnny loved the Lord and wanted to help in any way possible to get the good news of Jesus Christ out to the tribes of Vietnam. John, Jimmy, and Johnny would take doctors out to the villages to administer essential medical aid. Most often the U.S. Army or Air Force would supply a helicopter to send in a medical team.

Some readers might be surprised at hearing that the military was involved with aiding the people. The true story about Vietnam is that the American military did a tremendous amount of good for the people. After all, that is why they were there, to help them. These stories of aid get lost in some of the other unfortunate aspects of U.S. involvement in Vietnam.

Some of the most basic medical needs were performed. One time a dentist, with the help of John reassuring the people, extracted twenty-six teeth in an hour and a half. The tribesmen were very brave and took the extractions without any painkillers. John remembers a lot of blood and pus. The infections were unbelievable. But with the extractions and some antibiotics, people were healed.

It became almost routine after awhile. Military personnel from Da Lat would contact John, and he would set up the arrangements for delivering the medical team. John learned some minor procedures along the way. In some regions heavily affected by the war or some seasonal drought or flood that caused crop failure, John witnessed many of the signs of malnutrition. Kids with bloated bellies would come running up to their helicopters, filled with great excitement to see the team. John remembers pouring de-worming medicine down hundreds of people's throats. He remembers having to pinch their noses and lean their heads back to pour it down them. In spite of the rough nature of the medical procedures the tribal folks were amazingly trusting. John remembers, "It was nasty stuff, but it made them feel better."

Performing medical procedures for the tribal people as well as the Vietnamese was a challenge. They didn't believe in oral medications. They thought that for any medicine to work they had to have a shot. John remembers that sometimes they would have to shoot them with sugar water just to make them feel better about their treatment. John's ability to help the military personnel with interpretation and translation became providential to establishing an elaborate relationship that led to other ministry triumphs.

As his medical ministry quickly bloomed John saw the need for a more sophisticated medical facility for the tribal people. Many were dying unnecessarily from illnesses and conditions that were treatable if there were the proper facilities. Not only did they need medical help for diseases, but they also needed surgical facilities for those people who were injured from the war.

In Da Lat there was a military training facility and hospital, but it mostly served the Vietnamese and military casualties. The tribal people had nothing. So John felt compelled to create their own hospital. They had to call it a medical clinic, but it would be in every respect a hospital.

John set out to raise the funds needed to start the clinic. Of course his good friend Merv Rosell sent thousands of dollars. Other agencies, such as the Mennonite Central Committee, Food for the Hungry, and World Vision, donated money to see the clinic become a reality. He also sent back messages to the States to ask people to give money for this most worthy cause. He was able to put a selection of slides together showing the needs of the area, and people responded amazingly. In a very short time the clinic was up and running and staffed with doctors and nurses from the United Kingdom and North America.

John again was thrust into a responsibility that he didn't have the slightest bit of training for, but he took it just the same. His love for Christ and his love for the tribal people was all it took to be motivated. He became the director of the medical clinic in Da Lat. It was overwhelming at first trying to manage the budget, order supplies, and meet staffing needs and a host of crises that would arise daily. Even though John was not a doctor, the people always referred to him as Dr. John.

John's skills continued to be much in demand. The Mennonite Central Committee asked John to be their representative in the Central Highlands. They had food resources that could be delivered to the Da Lat airport to feed people when they needed something. John often unloaded bulgur wheat or rice from the airplanes himself.

All these duties gave John tremendous power and responsibility. He found himself praying for grace constantly. And to his amazement he found the strength and quick learning ability to handle each challenge.

Not only did this relief work save and improve the quality of life for hundreds of tribal people, but it gave John just that much more credibility. He was becoming nothing short of a folk hero. But John was careful not to let this folk admiration go to his head or get in the way of showing that it was Jesus' love that was providing for their needs. He was careful to show that it was because of God's care for them as a people that services were being provided. The food, the medical care, the shelter supplies, and whatever he had been used to help provide were ultimately supplied by God, and they should give Him the glory.

As the war continued to grow in intensity and the needs grew right along with it, the opportunities grew as well. John was in the enviable position of having the ear of the people. When there was time, Sau A, Jimmy, Johnny, and John were able to go into the villages and explain how Jesus loved them and gave His life for them. The fact that John had worked so tirelessly for their sakes won him the right to be heard. They were the beneficiaries, and the kingdom of God grew as a result.

With the increases in responsibility, village evangelism was difficult to fit in as he had done in the early days. But he was able to set up services wherever he was sent by the military or was delivering supplies. It worked out great. Many of the villages had developed so many converts that they could be considered Christian villages.

John was often host to important officials who came to visit South Vietnam. Anytime someone wanted to see what was going on in the Central Highlands, and more particularly among the Montagnards, they would call John and he would give them a tour. John recalls in particular two times he was such a host. Once, the senior province advisor (a U.S. civilian whose task was to advise the province chief) was sent to John for a tour of the villages in his area. On another occasion the ambassadors of Austria and Czechoslovakia came to see the work among the tribal people. John gave them one of his patented village tours.

He would first have to call the Air Force to arrange for a helicopter. Depending on how much time they had available he would fly the visitors to several villages. At the first stop he would show them a village that had few if any Christians. The village would show all the signs of being quite primitive. The people were dressed in little but a G-string, many were obviously malnourished, the villagers were scattered about performing all kinds of duties, and chickens and pigs were running freely throughout. The village had an air of disorganization. Most of the time the officials were interested in the effect of the relief efforts of USAID or some other government organization.

The visitors would see some help provided by the government, and they were at first impressed with the tribal culture and some of the efforts. In reality John was setting them up. He would then lead them on a tour of one of the predominantly Christian villages. When they arrived there were obvious differences. They immediately noticed the greater level of order, the church building which was the largest in the community, the people clearly healthier and happier. They were also better clothed. This was not an issue for John, and he never pushed having to change their cultural traits. They made these decisions on their own as they came to know more of God and His Word.

The visitors were indeed impressed. They were forced to recognize the effectiveness of John and missionaries from the Christian and Missionary Alliance in the area. John was able to explain that the credit needed to go the Lord. He was able to witness to the grace of God to many of these officials over the years. A U.S. Army colonel, who was a Christian, got his life right with the Lord upon seeing the difference in the villages and talking with John. The impact of the tribal visits showed him how devoted the tribal Christians were to Christ in the midst of their difficulties, so much that it put him to shame. He and John talked after they returned to his comfortable villa. He confessed that he had strayed away from the Lord and his priorities were out of balance. It touched his heart how these simple people had such a deep faith. He asked John to lead him in a prayer of rededication. He later became very involved in gospel work among American soldiers in Saigon.

John was always looking for ways to help the people for the long term, not just the short term. It was the philosophy that you can provide someone with fish and feed them for a day, or you can teach them to fish and you can feed them for a lifetime. The tribes were a combination of hunters and farmers, mostly farmers. However, their farming techniques lacked sophistication. Their common practice was to clear out an area of trees and then plant their crops and use up the nutrients in the soil quickly. After about three years they would move on to a new section of land and clear it off. The realities of the twentieth century were such that moving anyplace they wanted wouldn't work anymore. Especially in the middle of a war.

John decided that the best thing to do would be to start a technical training school. It was located about 50 km south of Da Lat and would train the tribal people in the use of modern agricultural techniques to maximize their yields and guide them to a better level of prosperity. In combination with the tech school, John and other missionaries set up a short-term Bible school to meet their spiritual needs in the same location.

It was a great way to train young people with new leadership skills for their communities to fulfill the economic needs as well as their church leadership needs. With the growing number of converts to Christ in the area there was always the demand for proper Bible training. They had the Scriptures translated into some of the languages, but by no means all. The people needed a sound foundation of biblical truth that would keep the Evil One at bay.

They were able to combine the technical school with a short-term Bible school in order to fill that need. Through the resources of the agencies that John had access to, as well as fund-raising in other mission societies represented in Vietnam, they were able to fund the staff and provide equipment for the entire school. They were able to use the abandoned Christian and Missionary Alliance school for missionaries' kids to house the school. It was an amazing accomplishment.

Through the ministry of Glenn Johnson, another Beacon Chapel missionary serving with Overseas Crusades, they were able to set up a very popular language school where the Vietnamese nationals living in Da Lat could learn English. Over five hundred people registered for these classes. They knew that learning English would likely open up better opportunities for them. The whole complex developed into a youth center for even more ministry.

In the span of ten years John had been able to be a big part of setting up a language school, organizing multiagency relief efforts, a technical agricultural school, short-term Bible schools, an international tour guide, and most of all, village evangelist. The days were full of activity and purpose. John had become a pioneer evangelist to the tribespeople of the Central Highlands. He had delivered the good news of Jesus the Lamb of God coming to this earth to die on the cross for the sins of all mankind, including the tribes of Vietnam. Some back home were calling him the apostle to the tribal people of Vietnam. Those financial supporters back home were getting their money's worth. Christ's church was growing, and the suffering of people was diminishing. John knew that all the praise had to go to God. He was deeply grateful for the opportunity to be used as he had been. But there was so much more to do.

As the year 1968 approached, the Vietnamese were beginning to have hopes of an end to the war. With the Americans deeply committed to preventing a communist takeover and some battlefield victories they believed the war might be over soon. Nothing could be further from the truth. The year 1968 was going to be the worst year yet in the war, and a pivotal time in American policy.

Chapter 7

The Tragedy of Tet

John and Jo left for the United States on missionary furlough in the fall of 1967. It's customary for overseas missionaries to be on the field for four years and return for one year to rest and to report to their supporting churches and friends. This furlough was anything but restful for the Newmans. They spent eleven of the twelve months of their furlough traveling. Most of their supporters were in the Pacific Northwest, but they had others around the entire country. They were busy from the start, making dramatic presentations that roused enthusiasm for the work of the Lord in Vietnam. John loved this part of missionary work almost as much as village evangelism. He loved telling Americans about how Jesus Christ changed the lives of many tribal people, how He delivered them from worshipping spirits and other sins that kept them in spiritual darkness. It was what "missions" was all about, and he was right in the middle of one of the greatest works of evangelism going on at that time. He reported that he had observed the war intensify as the years went on, but that the American presence was making a difference and was allowing missionaries more time to preach the gospel of Christ. In spite of the strong debate going on at the time over Vietnam, people were receptive to his message. In reality, most Americans favored support of South Vietnam, and Christians who knew about the evangelistic efforts were in favor of a policy that would allow that effort to continue. It was God's providence for John and Jo to be away from Vietnam during the winter of 1967–1968. The Lord was looking out for the Newmans in a special way, because Vietnam was soon to explode into a level of violence not yet seen in the war up to that point.

General Giáp (pronounced gee-yap) of the North Vietnamese forces developed a plan for an all-out assault on South Vietnam to take place during the Vietnamese New Year holiday known as Tet. It was customary to cease all hostilities and celebrate during the holiday. It was similar to our Christmas tradition. Giáp's goal was to strike all portions of South Vietnam in a surprise attack using North Vietnamese forces and Vietcong. The communist forces spent months secretly bringing arms into the towns and cities by hiding them in loads of farm products. The Ho Chi Minh Trail was teeming with activity. Thousands of communist forces were infiltrating the South to launch the offensive. The Tet Offensive was to be the last push to an overthrow of the government of South Vietnam.

South Vietnamese officials and American forces suspected that an offensive was coming, but they underestimated the magnitude of the plan. The mountain people's army, known as FULRO, a French acronym, had scouted all the way into Cambodia and reported that communist forces were staging war games there, apparently practicing for a major offensive. In late 1967 and early 1968 they also spotted them coming down the Ho Chi Minh Trail in record numbers, indicating that a huge offensive was imminent.

The Tet Offensive was to begin on January 30, 1968. The South Vietnamese assumed that the communists would honor the traditional holiday and perhaps attack shortly thereafter. They underestimated the numbers that would be involved, and they assumed too much when they counted on the communists honoring the cease-fire. Many military personnel were home on leave, celebrating the new year with their families and friends, and the whole country was left vulnerable.

The Vietcong forces that infiltrated the Central Highlands of South Vietnam, John's territory, attacked first on January 29. This was originally to be the attack day, but General Giáp tried to delay the attack to the 30th. The forces located in the interior, however, didn't get the message. This was devastating to the towns of Ban Me Thuot, Da Lat, and a few others. The towns and villages were celebrating with firecrackers and streamers and music. The people were in the streets, staying up late, celebrating with extra exuberance because they wanted so desperately to escape the realities of war. All of a sudden the loud noises in the street were amplified by ten with mortar rockets and real gunfire in an all-out assault on towns like Da Lat, Ban Me Thuot, and Phon Ron. South Vietnamese citizens were chaotically running for cover anyplace they could. Flashes of fire and flying metal made every step taken out in the open street a risk for anyone. The smell of exploding TNT was everywhere, and it was synonymous with the smell of death. Ashen smoke lingered all around, adding to the chaos. These towns had seen only sporadic fighting before, and now they were the centerpiece of a major military offensive. Hundreds of people were killed and thousands injured just because they were unsuspecting and had underestimated the over 100,000 communist troops that were involved.

The towns of the Central Highlands were first to see the magnitude of this new attack, and they suffered greatly. But because the other attacks were scheduled for the 30th, this gave the rest of the country a bit of warning as to what was in store for them. Had it not been for this error in communication the communist effort might have been much more devastating.

As the full impact of a nationwide, simultaneous attack by the communists began to set in, questions began to be asked. How could the communists pull off such a coordinated effort? Were we in any way winning this war? If so, how could we be so wrong about their strength? The Tet Offensive has become an enigma in American military history. Getting to the truth about what happened is no easy task. Most historians agree that the Tet Offensive, in spite of catching the U.S. off guard, was ultimately a great victory over the communist forces. There is credible evidence that the communists felt the same way too, and subsequently captured documents indicate that they recognized the defeat early and sought to rally their forces to continue the protracted-war strategy that they had adopted in previous years.

What America saw at home concerning the Tet Offensive was different from what the soldiers saw in Vietnam. The news media reported the capture of the American Embassy, street fighting in Saigon, the siege on Hue, and the ongoing attacks at Khe Sanh. Tet no doubt brought on the fiercest fighting of the war. American casualties reached record proportions, and the American dead numbered 250 a week. Tet challenged America's resolve to defend South Vietnam like no other single event. The amount of casualties and intensity of battle witnessed nightly on the news was becoming too much for the country to justify. Tet made most Americans decide that a pullout was going to be necessary. Even some of President Johnson's closest advisors were turning against the war effort.

From the American military perspective the U.S. and SVN armed forces defeated the communists handily, even though they were a great challenge. It is conservatively estimated that communist forces lost six times the number of dead and many more wounded compared with the friendly forces. But these facts were overlooked by the majority of Americans back home. Most wanted out of this war and saw no positive end in sight. It was an election year, and Vietnam was the number one issue in the nation. American sentiment about the war was affected even further by *Life* magazine publishing the pictures of all the Americans killed in just one week. It included over two hundred pictures of young, uniformed soldiers with a brief history of where they were from, their unit, their rank, and where they were killed. Flipping through the pages like a high school yearbook was a chilling experience for millions. It put Americans face-to-face with the real cost of this war. If Tet was a military victory for the U.S. and South Vietnamese forces in Vietnam, it turned out to be a political defeat in America.

John and Jo watched the oncoming storm of the Tet Offensive with great apprehension. They were in California at the World Vision headquarters when the offensive began. They had heard about FULRO's report of the enemy troops preparing for the offensive and knew that it was trustworthy. Their fellow missionaries in Da Lat were evacuated because the U.S. embassy recommended it, but several of their missionary friends further north in Ban Me Thuot stayed and assumed they could ride out the storm.

When John and Jo heard that the beginning of the offensive took place in the Central Highlands, their concerns doubled. These were their people. Their love for these people was deep, and it hurt them that they were so helpless. They watched the news on TV as often as it was on and called anyone whom they thought might have firsthand information as to the safety of the mountain people and their missionary colleagues. They were able to get bits and pieces of information, but it was unsatisfying. They needed to know more.

Watching the nightly TV news was a new experience for the Newmans. It was the first time they saw the war reported from the American media's position. They saw the war from a completely different point of view. They began to see the way many Americans were perceiving the war. They were skeptical of the reliability of the media and sought other sources for up-to-date information. Information was scarce, but they knew that the central region was a vulnerable place, and they also knew that the communists had a reputation for being very brutal. It spelled disaster.

John was grateful to God for His providential protection, but he couldn't just sit around and do nothing. He quickly made inquiries about the needs of the tribal people and the churches in the Central Highlands. As he got more information he went up and down the West Coast and parts of the East Coast raising money for the special needs of his people. He also got on Clay Cooper's radio broadcast to raise funds for what was called the Christian Emergency Fund. As usual, John's convincing manner and trustworthiness led to a considerable sum. Of course, Merv Rosell was faithful to contribute a large sum; in fact, he alone raised pledges of $10,000 for this new emergency.

In spite of the fact that he was on furlough, John felt he had to go back to Vietnam as soon as possible. Clay Cooper wanted to go along to report on the current situation in the country. By April 1968 things had died down from the offensive and it became safe to make the trip back. The American and South Vietnamese forces stopped the attack, and the war was resuming its pre-Tet mode. John and Clay had been in Vietnam together in the early fifties, but it was a drastically different country by 1968.

Many Christian folks who followed the careers of John and Clay must have felt they needed to go back as well, because it was no problem raising their airfare. They soon found themselves on a long trip over the Pacific in anticipation of witnessing the full impact of modern war and in hopes of helping as many as possible. When they arrived at Tan Son Nhat Airport in Saigon, even from their airplane window they immediately noticed a heightened level of security. Barbed wire and sandbagged bunkers were all around, and there were soldiers everywhere you turned. Along with the security measures, the next sight was the number of destroyed buildings. The gunfire that had rattled through the streets and the artillery that had pounded the air with a deafening roar in Saigon just weeks earlier had gone quiet. There was little sound of gunfire except for some occasional rounds taking place far outside the city.

As they reached their quarters at the World Vision guesthouse in Saigon they quickly made preparations to tour the city and interview as many people as possible. Their plan was to get a feel for the state of affairs in Saigon and then move north to the Central Highlands where John's people were. They toured the city with the help of some guides and observed the aftermath of Tet. Saigon had been relatively untouched by the war up to that point. It was astonishing to John to see some of the destruction, but he was actually relieved it wasn't worse. From all the reports in the U.S. it sounded like all of Saigon was affected, but in reality much of it was left untouched. Along with their tour they interviewed as many people as they could to get the human touch to their story. After a few days they were ready to report their findings, so they set up their recording equipment for a broadcast on Clay's nationwide radio program.

In Clay's silvery baritone voice and dramatic style he began their broadcast to the States describing the current scene in Saigon. It was evening, and the air was still hot and sticky but more comfortable than earlier in the day. A faint scent of smoke hung in the air from all the battles and fires of the previous months. In order to give the listening audience a feel for warlike conditions, Clay started the show with the sounds of rapid gunfire and explosions from the recent siege in Hue up north. To listeners it sounded like they were in the middle of heavy fire. In fact there was a calm all over

Saigon that hadn't existed for years. John and Clay shared the microphone and quickly clarified the fact that they were hearing the sounds of a battle that had taken place weeks earlier. They began relaying back and forth in concert the recent events in Saigon and what they had seen and heard in those first few days.

The reoccurring theme from their interviews had to do with the Vietnamese concern for American support. John relayed the messages that he had heard over and over again. The Vietnamese people were concerned that in the wake of the Tet Offensive and the subsequent political fallout, the United States was about to "sell out" the country of South Vietnam for a compromise solution, a compromise that would let the communists have an open door for ultimate victory. According to John's interviews with the citizens of the South, they were actually more confident than ever that they could win the war. What an irony when the U.S. at the same time was losing its resolve. John expressed that he hoped that the U.S. wouldn't let the people of South Vietnam down.

Many in the South were very grateful for American involvement. Some owed their very lives to the Americans. There are probably many stories to demonstrate this point, but the case of Madame Hue is one story of sacrifice and raw courage by ordinary American soldiers. John and Clay heard firsthand how American soldiers saved the lives of Madame Hue, a respected Vietnamese citizen, and her children. She was among the higher society of South Vietnam and was said to have had the ear of President Nguyen Van Thieu.

John and Clay were amazed as this petite, attractive widow, dressed in the typical white silk gown down to her ankles and pants underneath, relayed the story. She was at her home when the assault on Saigon took place on January 30. A platoon of American soldiers happened to be patrolling right by her home when the Vietcong attacked and fired one of their rockets at her house. It's not clear whether the communists knew to target their rockets at her home, or whether they were trying to hit the American soldiers. It is possible that they may have known her to be close to the government and singled out her home for the attack. Either way, American soldiers found themselves in her yard, hiding behind her rock fence, doing everything possible to protect her and her five children and stay alive themselves. The battle raged for several hours and the Americans were sitting ducks to the shelling. After hours of intense battle, eighteen Americans had lost their lives and ten more were wounded.

Madame Hue was deeply moved and wept quietly as she told how these young men had come all around the world to give their lives for her, right in her front yard. John and Clay couldn't help but see the parallel with the work of Jesus Christ through his missionaries. They both hoped that the people of Vietnam would come to see that the sacrifice of Jesus on the cross was even greater than those soldiers.

Madame Hue also mentioned how she was opposed to the idea of a coalition government with the VC, or National Liberation Front, as they called themselves. This was an idea being kicked around among the Democrats back in America. "You can't trust the VC. I know, I was one of them for twenty years," she said. When she was younger she had believed in Marxist ideology and felt it would save her country. But as time went on, she saw the true nature of communism and began to turn away from it. She later came to believe that the hope of her nation was in democracy and a market economy. Her appeal was convincing. She felt that the South Vietnamese had a new resolve and confidence that they could fight the war themselves and that the communists were losing the war for the hearts and minds of the people.

John and Clay were deeply impressed with the testimonies they had heard so far. They were anxious, however, to get up to Ban Me Thuot, where it was reported that great devastation had taken place and that several American missionaries had lost their lives during the Tet Offensive. They caught a flight to Ban Me Thuot and stayed at a military compound where it was safe. As soon as they got off the plane, they saw that everything they had heard was true, and understated, to say the least. The area missionaries had homes located together in a prosperous neighborhood in Ban Me Thuot. They drove immediately to the row of missionary homes.

Ban Me Thuot is one of South Vietnam's larger cities, but it is located in the mountains and therefore closer to the mountain people. The Rade (pronounced ra-day) tribe lived in the area, and several pioneer works had been started by Christian and Missionary Alliance missionaries decades earlier. As John and Clay drove around the bend where the row of houses was, all they saw was rubble where once their friends had homes. They were stunned at the total destruction of these homes. They knew that in the rubble were stories of horror for their friends who died in the Lord's service. John had been in these homes several times throughout his career in Vietnam. He immediately pictured those sweet times of fellowship as if those memories were ghosts hanging over the debris. A sense of sadness was beginning to set in as they began to assess the true loss. The whole adventure was becoming an odyssey of one tragic story after another.

They met with some survivors who told them about the day when the bombs began to fall. John and Clay wanted to know everything, but they first wanted to know what happened to their missionary friend Caroline Griswold. The case of Caroline Griswold is a story of one of God's servants who was willing to serve the Savior at any cost. She was an attractive, classy woman from White Plains, New York. Her love for the Lord had given her the desire to serve Christ anywhere He would lead her. She was led to the pine-forested mountains of Vietnam in Ban Me Thuot to work among the loinclothed, primitive Rade people.

Caroline's prim and proper upbringing gave her little experience in being out in the wild country. In fact, she had never even been camping before she set out for Vietnam. But after her Bible training was completed and her missionary call took her halfway around the world, she was soon spending her days out on the trails and streams establishing a gospel witness to the villages of the Rade people. She loved the people with all her heart, and they loved her. John was always struck by the fact that in spite of being out in the aboriginal territory of Vietnam she always dressed in stylish clothes like she had just gone out and bought them at Macy's.

She and most of the other missionaries were alerted to the upcoming Tet Offensive, but they decided to hunker down and ride it out. They had survived so many crises before, and other conditions brought on by the war. Caroline and her father were hiding in their home. They thought it would be a safe place during the attack, but they were wrong. No one knows whether communist forces particularly targeted the homes on missionary row, but several of the homes were hit with their firepower. Thunderous explosions rattled the walls and floor of their home and shook the house like an earthquake. They felt that they were safest in the house, but as the shells came closer they considered making a break for it somewhere else. Before they made their way out, a Russian-made 122 mm rocket hit their two-story house. It was bigger than the earlier mortar and grenade explosions and thundered with a deeper and more earth-shattering sound. It was a direct hit and brought down the concrete-and-steel-reinforced structure like a house of cards. Caroline's father was killed instantly, and Caroline was hit with and pinned underneath debris from the house. She suffered from some lacerations and serious internal injuries from being hit with hundreds of pounds of concrete in several parts of her body.

When the dust of the explosion settled Caroline looked for signs of her father. She saw his still limbs sticking out from a large piece of concrete. She knew he was dead, but she shook his leg just in case there was a response. He didn't respond. The tragedy of the moment had not sunk in, and instinct kicked in. She knew that she had to take care of herself if she was going to live. The U.S. military saw she was hurt, picked her up, and delivered her to a field hospital. Her external injuries seemed less serious to the hospital staff than some of their other cases, and her internal injuries went undetected. Caroline was not one to complain, and she didn't know herself the extent of her injuries. She died within three days. It was an agonizing death that could likely have been prevented had she been able to receive better care.

Caroline's main ministry was with the youth among the Rade tribal people. She had a wonderful ministry going before she died. Many kids were coming to Christ, and they adored her. Caroline represented the very light of the gospel and the true love of Jesus Christ. The news of her death was traumatic to the Rade people. If the communists targeted missionaries and pastors, it was because they believed that their deaths would demoralize the people. This strategy worked with cruel and heartbreaking effectiveness. In fact, the people were so emotionally devastated by Caroline's death that they would weep openly at the drop of a hat. They were truly demoralized and hurt, but they remained faithful to follow the Savior to whom she had introduced them.

On the day that the Griswolds were killed by the rocket attack, other missionaries were peering out their windows wondering what to do. Ed and Ruth Thompson and Bob Zeimer decided to make a break for it to the garbage pit near their homes. They thought they might be able to use it as a bunker of sorts for protection. Since the chance of surviving the attack in their homes was diminishing, they quickly ran for the pit. In a mad rush to turn it into a bunker they moved the scrap wood, bamboo, and metal sheeting over their heads. They hunkered down and prayed earnestly for God to protect them. They didn't care that they were kneeling in and surrounded by rotting vegetables and other stinking debris.

The shelling continued all around them. Though they couldn't look out and see what was being destroyed, their homes were coming down and the Christian and Missionary Alliance compound was being destroyed. The two chapels were gutted with fire, and the medical clinic and infirmary were completely destroyed. Each explosion sent a shot of fear into them all, but it wasn't a hysterical fear. They were holding one another's hands for mutual support and a sign of their oneness in their unshakable faith. They soon heard the voices of Vietcong soldiers coming closer, firing their automatic rifles. They prayed that they wouldn't be noticed, but they were.

A communist soldier shouted a sarcastic phrase in Vietnamese and then opened fire into the garbage pit. Many of the bullets hit the three of them, and screams of pain and pleas for mercy went up in the midst of the sound of the automatic fire. In order to make sure they were all dead, the VC threw a grenade into the garbage pit and instantly killed all three. Ed and Ruth Thompson were missionaries to the Rade in Ban Me Thuot and were just in the process of relocating to another part of the Central Highlands. Bob Zeimer was a great preacher and teacher who was considered the grandfather among the Rade people for his pioneer evangelistic work among them.

The garbage pit was an ignoble place for them to die. Certainly they didn't belong in such a place. These precious jewels sought refuge by covering themselves with whatever scraps they could and by covering themselves with prayer. They couldn't run to a place with better cover, because the attack was too intense. Mortar rounds were exploding all around, and the air was full of flying metal from the communists' guns. For years these servants had been protected from this kind of fighting, but now it was surrounding them in an inescapable destiny. For whatever reason, God in His infinite wisdom allowed the Vietcong success that day, and five missionaries died.

John and Clay visited the garbage pit and the very spot where the attack took place. It was difficult to reconstruct the scene that day with the debris scattered every which way. They were struck with a myriad of emotions: anger, sorrow, disgust, fear, and sympathy for those who lost their loved ones. Their hearts were broken as they heard of even more horrors brought on by the communist forces.

In one case the communists captured four Rade youngsters and a pastor of one of the village churches near Ban Me Thuot. Two of the youngsters were children of the pastor. They shot the four children in sight of the rest of the village and took the pastor away. The village was horrified and terrified by the actions of the communists. They didn't know what would come next. It put their faith in Christ to its greatest test so far in the war.

The pastor, with his hands harshly tied behind his back, was marched away from the village. They were taking him to Hanoi to suffer some unimaginable imprisonment up there. They dragged him up and down through the arduous mountains of the interior. Abused and malnourished for weeks, he managed to escape his captors before they reached Hanoi. He walked for days, braving the elements of the mountains and the dangers of tigers and snakes. He floated down streams and managed with the depleted energy he had left to make it back to Ban Me Thuot. He stumbled into town the very day John and Clay arrived, after two months and twenty-three days in captivity. He was the talk of the town. He had lost thirty pounds and was extremely weak, but was able to tell his story. Everyone was praising the Lord for His mercy in returning their pastor to them.

Later that day after examining the garbage pit and hearing the story of the captive pastor, John and Clay made a solemn visit to the graves of Ed and Ruth Thompson. The visit served as a brief memorial for them. John knew them both very well. John and Clay mused on the fact that these servants gave their lives in service for Jesus. They could have lived their lives in comfort and safety back in America, but they were driven first by a love for Jesus Christ, and secondly a love for the people. It was a sobering thought.

They walked up through the row of homes where the missionaries had lived. The bombed-out houses were a shocking scene. They came to the backyard of the Thompsons' home where their graves lay. They stood over them in somber thought and prayed to the Lord. As Clay looked around, he saw Ruth's passport on the ground. It was partially destroyed, but with it was a piece of paper with some writing on it. Clay picked it up and in the Rade language read the simple phrase "opposite shore." He found out it was a way to communicate the message to the Rade that going to be with the Lord when you die is like going to the "opposite shore." He wasn't sure when Ruth had written this, but he noted in one of his broadcasts that she had her hope set on Jesus and ultimately was sitting by His side. As he looked around the grave site some more, he noticed some pages from a hymnal, blown around by the wind. Clay was compelled to read the words, as they now had great significance to him and the Rade whom the Thompsons loved. The words to the familiar hymn went as follows:

> *Be not dismayed whate'er betide, God will take care*
> *of you;*
> *Beneath His wings of Love abide, God will take care*
> *of you.*
> *Through days of toil when heart doth fail, God will*
> *take care of you;*

*When dangers fierce your path assail, God will take
   care of you.*
*No matter what may be the test, God will take care
   of you;*
*Lean, weary one, upon His breast, God will take care
   of you.*

Clay sensed he was on holy ground as he stood by the graves marked with simple crosses in the red soil of the Ban Me Thuot region. These were brethren in Christ who took Him at His word to be ambassadors, to go and preach the gospel and make disciples to the very ends of the earth. It was a day Clay would never forget. Later that night John and Clay relayed the day and all of its impact on them to their radio audience.

There was other work to be done. John's trip back to South Vietnam during his furlough was to distribute the funds he had been able to raise in response to the many needs brought on by the Tet Offensive. He first moved around the region making a mental account of the many needs and began distributing some of the goods that they bought with the funds they had raised. The first priority in giving aid was to assist the pastors and churches that experienced damage. The pastors often had no other means of support, and the churches destroyed in the war needed to be repaired. The Christian people were still meeting to worship the Lord in spite of their bombed-out villages and churches. In fact, the recent offensive caused more people to attend services. The faithful nationals were witnessing to hope in the Lord Jesus Christ. New converts were coming to the Lord, but there was also a state of fear beginning to creep into the churches as the stories of the communists' brutalities were making their way around.

John had $1,000 for immediate needs and bought food for the Christian tribal people as well as about ten pastors.

The South Vietnamese government and U.S. agencies were able to take care of some of the needs, but not all of them. John was mindful of the Scripture that reads, "Do good to all people, and especially to those who are of the household of faith," so this helped set the priorities in giving aid. Merv Rosell and many individuals had contributed to this special fund, called the Christian Emergency Fund, and Clay used his radio program to drum up contributors. The money was still pouring in even as they were in Vietnam. The up-to-date broadcasts they were making from the country touched the hearts of hundreds of people. It was an effective strategy, and the people of the Central Highlands were the beneficiaries.

Ban Me Thuot saw the full impact of the Tet Offensive. In a two-and-a-half-block area there were six hundred bodies in the street, victims of the communist attack. It was one story after another. Missionary Hank Blood of Wycliffe Bible Translators and Esther Olson, a nurse with the Christian and Missionary Alliance, were captured by the VC and taken to Hanoi. They both died along the way, likely from dysentery. Betty Mitchell, another missionary, was kidnapped as well and taken to Hanoi, but survived the ordeal and was released in 1973 when the peace settlement was signed.

The Tet Offensive left thousands in a state of terror. The fear of death, injury, captivity, or torture was almost too much for the people to bear, and the fear was becoming contagious. The tribal people were heavily hit by the series of attacks and the missionaries saw an unprecedented number killed. The Vietnamese citizens were devastated. Not one group was spared, and it tested the faith of the Christians more than at any time in their lives. They hung on to the promises of God such as Matthew 28:20, "Lo, I am with you always, even to the end of the age," and John 10:27–28, "My sheep hear My voice, and I know them, and they follow Me; and I give eternal life to them, and they will never perish; and no one will snatch them out of the My hand." These words comforted them.

John reported that several missionaries had been gripped with fear and were afraid to venture much beyond their homes. He understood but knew he couldn't respond the same way. He had to keep going in spite of the recent tragedies in order to have a ministry.

After being fully briefed in Ban Me Thuot, John and Clay traveled down to Da Lat. This was John's territory, and he was anxious to see his people. He had heard that the city of Da Lat had been embroiled in twelve days of fierce fighting. John hurried to his home to see the condition it was in. His heart sank as he came upon the beautiful French villa that had been John and Jo's comfortable home for years. It was still standing, but all the windows were completely blown out, along with some doors and several pieces of ceiling and wall that had come off. As he came to the front door it was apparent that the home was unlivable. He toured the home and found that it had been looted. Everything of value was taken: his tiger pelt, other hunting trophies, their solid hardwood dining room table and china cabinet, and every electrical and plumbing fixture in the house. It was gutted and unlivable. He knew it would change things when they came back from furlough for their next term. He asked around about what happened and found out that ironically the house was damaged by an American bomb that was dropped about a block away.

John and Clay got a sense of the disaster that had taken place in Vietnam from Tet. For the Vietnamese it had a near-apocalyptic overtone, and in fact many Christians in Vietnam began to believe that the Lord must be very near His return, since they were at the brink of disaster. They saw how the communists, without conscience, would kill the people and throw their bodies into the streets to terrorize the community. They thought that nothing but the end of the world could be near. They wondered how things could get any worse. With the obvious persecution of Christians by the communist forces they felt that this confirmed their notion. But it wasn't the end. It was another in a long line of atrocities that have been all too common in human history.

Reports and rumors of brutality were flying everywhere. The number of tribal villages that suffered are too numerous to give all the accounts. Displaced Montagnards were scattered throughout the city of Da Lat and living a nomadic existence throughout the countryside. The VC had targeted the mountain people in many of their attacks during the Tet Offensive. The focus on the mountain people seemed to be in part ethnic hatred and in part a political reaction to their tendency to support the Americans. One such attack took place at two villages that were located next to each other just south of Da Lat.

The two villages were Koho-speaking and located one down the hill from the other. It all started at 2 a.m. when the VC started shelling the two villages with Russian rockets and mortars. The villagers awakened from their sleep in a state of panic and disorientation. Longhouses were being destroyed all around them in flashes of yellow light as bodies and body parts were strewn over the red dirt. After the initial rocket attack the VC guerrillas came in and killed everything in sight. Almost every man, woman, and child was shot or stabbed on the spot. The villagers were helpless to defend themselves. The state of confusion that erupted left only a few villagers to escape into the forest in hopes of eluding the attackers. Most were separated from their loved ones fleeing for their own lives. After the attack was over only a few villagers had survived.

After the local missionaries reported the massacre the U.S. military responded by sending in a team to investigate what happened. A Colonel Michaels and some other officers from the army flew in by helicopter a few days after the attack. The village looked still and abandoned from the air, so they landed with caution, assuming that the VC had gone. In reality it was an ambush. The communists immediately attacked and killed all but one captain and one other officer in the group, whom they led into the forest about 2 kilometers. The captain was a well-respected Christian man with eight children. The two officers were found two weeks later badly mutilated. The terror these men experienced can only be imagined by the wounds that they had suffered. Both had their eyes gouged out, one had his arms chopped off at the elbow, and both of their faces were completely mutilated beyond recognition. The captain was identified by the well-read New Testament found inside his vest pocket, which John had given him months earlier.

To illustrate how tragic this was for the villagers, Bob Henry, a CMA missionary who was working with the Vietnamese, was asked to go in four days after the ambush on the officers. The military needed an interpreter. When they reached the village there were two pigs and one dog left alive. The stench was nearly unbearable. However, there was one sign of life. A small girl about four years old was found alive. Her name was Ma Thai, and she had been shot in the thigh. The bullet traveled through her pelvic bone and pierced her lower intestines and sciatic nerve, leaving her paralyzed, lying there for five days.

The army was able to airlift the child to the Da Lat hospital. She unfortunately ended up in the charity ward. Being low in priority because she was apparently orphaned and a tribal girl, she was neglected at the hospital. Bob was touched by the toughness of this little girl and insisted that she get moved to a paying ward and hopefully receive better attention. It helped some, but they were losing her. They eventually did surgery on her intestinal tract because it was oozing stool and causing infection. The first surgery was unsuccessful, but then they performed a colostomy. That was more effective, and the child began to get better.

The girl's mother miraculously escaped and survived the attack but had assumed her daughter was dead when she saw that she was hit. Bob sought to find the mother and received a tip that some of the people had been evacuated to a hospital in Phan Thiet, south of Da Lat near the coast. Every day Ma Thai would look up at Bob and say, "Have you found my mother yet?" So he was motivated to do what he could to help this little girl. When he got to the hospital at Phan Thiet he just went through the hospital shouting the mother's name, hoping that someone would respond. He saw someone raise her hand and point to the woman in the bed across from her. He said, "Are you Ma Thai's mother?" and she began to cry and shook her head, unable to speak. Bob told her that Ma Thai was alive and recovering from a very serious injury, and they rejoiced together.

The war was full of stories of tragedy, and also many miracles of mercy. The Tet Offensive simply intensified those experiences for almost everyone in Vietnam. John and Clay discovered that many people who had been putting their trust in spirits, sacrifices, Buddhism, socialism, or whatever else were beginning to reevaluate their source of hope and were turning to the risen Lord Jesus. Churches were filling and evangelism efforts were seeing more converts throughout the country. But the offensive and its aftermath showed that time might be running out for the little country of South Vietnam.

The trip was emotionally and physically exhausting for John and Clay. At the same time it had an invigorating effect on them, because it underscored the urgency to do whatever they could in spreading the good news of Jesus Christ in Vietnam. They had been gone for about a month, and they were excited to get back home to the States to join their families. They were full of many stories, and the folks back home would be very interested in hearing about their first-hand experience.

They couldn't help but see that the communist forces and communism in general were truly a serious evil in Southeast Asia. All the propaganda aside, they witnessed time and time again the disrespect for human life demonstrated by the NVA and VC forces. It was a pattern of actions, not the exception.

As for the American military personnel, it was quite the contrary. From John's experience in the country over most of the war he observed that they were extremely helpful to the Vietnamese and tribal people. The experience that John had and the reports of the Vietnamese and tribal people were that U.S. servicemen avoided as many civilian casualties in their bombing raids and patrol missions as was possible. It was disheartening to know that the victory of Tet for the government forces was being reduced to a defeat by America losing its resolve and perhaps laying the people of South Vietnam open to disaster.

As John and Clay concluded their trip they took with them the many stories of tragedy and hope. The outcome of the war would affect the continuation of missionary efforts all across Southeast Asia. They came home with a definite sense of urgency, but they knew they would battle the perceptions of the war in the mind of the average American.

The politics of Vietnam was a complex truth. And the truth that they knew about the war would likely change few Washington politicians or, for that matter, the average American's view. They knew that the door was wide open to the gospel, and they wanted to take full advantage of that open door as long as they could. When they returned they spread the stories out of Vietnam to whoever would listen and care. They were able to raise more money for the rebuilding of churches and food for the starving and displaced. They had been used of God to "rescue the perishing and care for the dying," and they rested in that knowledge. They had been a part of something great, and it thrilled their hearts as they boarded their plane in Saigon to return to the States.

Chapter 8

Coming Home

Furlough for the Newmans was an exciting time to share with their supporters all the great things that Jesus was doing in Vietnam in spite of the horrible war. The testimonies of the scores of tribal people who had given their hearts to Christ were a great encouragement to Christians in America. The cause of world evangelism was making great inroads in Southeast Asia. Some of it was happening at the faithful hands of John Newman. By the time John and Jo had reached the end of their yearlong furlough they were anxious to get back to the beautiful mountains of Da Lat. They enjoyed being able to reach their full financial support from various churches and individuals. They were also able to recruit a host of new prayer warriors to back them up as they prepared to return to the dangerous land of their ministry.

When it was time to return to Vietnam in December 1968 John and Jo flew into a much more secure Saigon. The heat was a nice change from the wintry conditions of Spokane, but still too hot and humid for comfort. They quickly made their way back to Da Lat. It was bittersweet to enter the city, because Jo saw for the first time their French villa which had been destroyed. From a distance it appeared that it could be their home once again with a few repairs, but as she got closer and looked inside it was clear that wouldn't be possible.

She was heartsick at seeing the destruction. The villa had been her home for years, and it was full of wonderful memories. They both reflected on the memories that home held for them. When John went upstairs to examine the damage he recalled the time that his pet gibbon, Hopalong Cassidy, had grabbed John's underwear and put it over his head. It was one of the funniest things John had ever seen. When he went to retrieve his private attire from the gibbon it leapt out the second-story window in a backwards flip. John thought for sure the fall would kill him, but he had nonchalantly grabbed a telephone wire on the way down, breaking his fall, and then scampered away. The memory brought a grin, but also a sense of sadness at knowing he and Jo would not be able to enjoy this home any longer. It marked the beginning of several changes that would have to be made.

They stayed their first night at the home of some missionary friends who were taking care of their big dog, Tipi. Tipi immediately recognized John and greeted him with the uncontrollable excitement that only a pet dog can give. That night as they tried to sleep, they heard shooting on a nearby hill just moments from where they were staying. It was unnerving, and a clear sign that Da Lat was not the safe haven it once was. A significant military base was located in Da Lat, so the chances of them getting hit were slim, but there was always the possibility that a random mortar round could be sent their way. With the communists more aggressive than ever, there were few "safe" places in South Vietnam.

After spending the night with their friends they began their move to a new location. They had to move to the upper floor of the abandoned Christian and Missionary Alliance school for the children of missionaries. It was comfortable, but not nearly as nice and accommodating as their previous home. However, within a few weeks Jo had converted the stark, abandoned rooms into a comfortable and inviting home, an expression and extension of her personality.

Jo had developed a wonderful ministry of hospitality while John pursued his evangelism/relief worker/administrator ministry. There was hardly a time when someone wasn't being entertained at the Newmans' home. The dining table was often filled with special guests. Jo had her own staff: a cook and groundskeeper. Because Da Lat was located at such a temperate climate, many missionaries from around the country made Da Lat a vacation site. The Newmans had an open invitation to such guests. The size of their home made it possible for guests to stay for days without interfering with the Newmans' privacy. Besides, they loved the company and Christian fellowship they enjoyed together. There were fewer joys greater to the Newmans than fellowshipping in Christ with other missionaries from around the country.

The guests were not only missionaries, but also dignitaries from around the country and even the world. The Czech and Austrian diplomats mentioned previously, American officials from USAID and U.S. Operations Mission (USOM), and representatives from various relief agencies that John worked with all came to stay and eat at the Newmans' home. Jo was a master at making people feel welcome. She often was overshadowed by John's ministry, but she was the quiet strength and support so needed by a man serving the Lord.

John's ministry had to change somewhat upon his return. The communists were keeping up the pressure throughout the country. In the old days John could travel much more freely, even into the night. Now, due to curfews and safety reasons, he had to be back from his journeys before night fell.

To work among the tribes was particularly dangerous, because it meant traveling on unprotected roads or trails.

John was brave but not foolish when it came to venturing out to the mountain villages. He developed a system of determining the safety of making a particular trip which worked well for him. John did not want the fear of harm to paralyze his ministry, so he sought ways to be as active as possible without being foolhardy.

He would first talk to the mountain people to see if they knew whether there were VC in the area. Their intelligence was the most reliable to John. They would sometimes overestimate the numbers if they were particularly afraid, but for the most part they knew what was going on. Next, he would ask Vietnamese military officials in the area. After that he would ask the American military. If all three agreed that it was safe to travel, then he would go ahead and make a trip. To say the least, it was a much more risky business getting the gospel out to people in the mountains in the post-Tet days.

John spent the first few months getting around to greet the various villages he had worked in before. He also had to step up his relief operations to continue assisting displaced village people. It was exciting for him to be among his people once again, and he loved preaching in Koho.

He remembered one service in particular. It was shortly after his return and not far from Da Lat. He arrived at the village a few hours early, so he stepped out into the woods for a few minutes to pray and make a few last preparations for his message. While he was praying for Jesus to give him the words that would be delicious on the ears of the tribal folks, a mile down the road an old man was being stopped by three NVA soldiers. He was on his way to the village for the service, and the NVA soldiers began asking him what the "long-nosed American" was doing in their village. The old man told them he was a preacher of the gospel. It was the first time John had heard that he had a long nose. They talked with the man more and asked if he would ask the long-nosed American to pray for them. The soldiers were sick and tired and lonesome for home. They showed respect for the "unknown God" and figured John might have a special "in" with the man upstairs.

John did pray for them, not that they would have success in their mission, but that they might see the light of the gospel and that God would have compassion on them. He knew that many NVA were conscripted. Not all NVA soldiers were communists or willing to fight for this cause. It was rumored that the NVA officers chained lower-ranking soldiers to their artillery pieces so they couldn't run. This would often leave them wide open to American air bombardment and certain death. John prayed for their souls before it was too late.

It was a profound experience for John, because he had never considered praying for the communists. It gave him a new perspective, and he prayed more often for the salvation of the communist troops. He found a love in his heart that he hadn't felt in a long time, a love that only Jesus can give. He knew it was the love of Jesus when he was able to love his enemies. He admits having harsh feelings for all communists because he saw them bring only death and terror and lies to the people he loved so much. But as he prayed, the words of Romans 12:14 came to him: "Bless those who persecute you; bless and do not curse." If he didn't pray for them, who would? If no one prayed for them, who would be willing to share the life-changing news of Jesus dying for their sins? This one experience gave John a new insight into the depth of the love of God.

Because John found himself more in Da Lat than he used to be before Tet, he was able to develop a ministry to the American military. He would get to know the personnel there and invite them to his home or to play basketball. He was also able to get them to fly him to some villages from time to time in their helicopters. It was a good relationship, and the gospel was furthered by it. Fellow missionary Glenn Johnson also set up a ministry to serve the American soldiers. Part of his ministry was located in Saigon in the hospitals treating those who were wounded in battle. In 1969 he was able to report that two thousand young men had come to a saving knowledge of Jesus Christ in the hospital ministry alone.

John also picked up his ministry with the technical school and the Bible institute in Nha Trang. He was constantly recruiting kids to get involved with either ministry so they could become more grounded in the Word and more economically independent.

In spite of the opportunity for gospel work, many people, including the Christians, were stricken with fear. The communists used fear as one of their greatest tools. It wasn't uncommon for people to dig holes underneath their beds and hide there all night. Even Sau A, the great spiritual leader of the tribes, was deeply affected. He was the tribal elder and the rock of the people, and even he was losing his courage.

His fear became paralyzing after an incident in Da Lat in 1970. The Vietnamese pastors had been attending a seminar on psychological warfare in Da Lat one summer. This seminar helped train a cadre to combat the efforts of the communists to wage psychological warfare on them. The pastors were considered the leaders of their villages. The communists figured that they could strike a huge blow to the morale of the people if they attacked this training center. They infiltrated the grounds in Da Lat near the military base and murdered twenty-three chaplains from around the country in a savage attack. It was a horrifying blow to the Christian brothers and sisters as well as the Buddhists.

With Sau A, the greatest leader among the tribal churches, in a state of fear himself, fear began to spread to the local believers. Sau knew that it was logical to be afraid after all that had happened, but he also knew that it was infecting others. John quietly counseled Sau, but he also knew that the Lord had to do the work in Sau's heart. As time went on, Sau began to find greater courage and resumed his travels around the country to minister to his people.

Other atrocities took place that contributed to the fear of the people. The village called Da Me suffered a serious attack in the post-Tet assaults. Da Me was actually five villages in one that had been relocated after being pushed out of their original land by the VC. They went through the village systematically and killed all the teachers, leaders, and professional people. They took two young men that they had murdered and hung their bodies in the doorway of the newest church in the village.

This macabre scene was designed to terrorize the surviving villagers. The scene worsened as dogs from the village came and ate the flesh off the bodies as they hung in the doorway of the church. It sickened and discouraged the people. John went down to that village to preach shortly after that, and in spite of the good attendance there was a sadness over them. John saw it in their eyes. He spoke there several times and it was always the same.

These tragedies were a part of everyday life in Vietnam. In order to keep a good sense of perspective and not get depressed by all the grief around him, John figured out ways to find pleasure. It was not all hard work and no play for John. He made a habit of playing basketball whenever he could. There were always opportunities to play, because of the South Vietnamese military school and U.S. military base located right in Da Lat. Whenever he could, he would get involved in a pickup game and mix it up with the guys.

He took the game of volleyball to the tribal people and taught them the rudiments of the game. They loved it. It was a bit awkward to play volleyball on a dirt court with uneven ground, but they managed. The biggest problem was seeing the ball go out of bounds and roll down a steep hill a thousand feet or so. It was a long hike back up the hill. It was a lot of fun and even opened up several opportunities.

Overseas Crusades had a traveling basketball team known as Venture for Victory, made up of college all-stars who wanted to serve the Lord by playing their game. They traveled around the world playing exhibition basketball games and sharing their testimonies. John was able to get them to come to Da Lat to play against the American GIs. It was a fun game, but the GIs were no match for the select team.

John was able to develop a tribal team to play the Vietnamese or the ethnic Chinese in special games. It would always draw a crowd, and the Chinese and Vietnamese would bet on the outcome. The tribal kids were always shorter than their opponents, but they often won. John loved to showcase the tribal team's terrific eye-hand ability because they were so often looked down upon in Vietnam.

The mixture of work and pleasure was something John has always been able to do. In fact, he would tell you he couldn't tell the difference between the two. His work was his pleasure, and his basketball was simply pleasurable exercise. It was important to have some fun in a land full of war and uncertainty. As time moved on, those pleasures yielded to limitations brought on by the war.

Things began to change in Vietnam during the first year back from furlough. Richard Nixon became president and began his Vietnamization program. This was a plan to turn increasing portions of the war effort over to the South Vietnamese. American troop strength was at its highest in 1969, around 550,000 total. The election of 1968 seemed to prove that most Americans wanted out of Vietnam sooner or later. The Paris Peace Talks with the communists were stalled, and Nixon tried to continue pressure on the North and at the same time diminish U.S. involvement to an eventual pullout. Nixon referred to his goal as "peace with honor," and most Americans believed that it was possible.

Domestic issues were beginning to take priority over the war in Vietnam. The country had suffered a devastating year in 1968, starting with the Tet Offensive, followed by Dr. Martin Luther King Jr's assassination, race riots around the country, Bobby Kennedy's assassination, riots in the streets of Chicago at the Democratic National Convention, peace marches, Black Panthers, Weathermen, and more. It seemed that the country was coming apart. Sympathy for the threatened South Vietnamese people was fading rapidly, to say the least.

Any policy change would have a direct effect on the way missionaries could operate in Vietnam. For the most part Nixon's policy had a positive impact on the South Vietnamese, who interpreted Nixon's resolve to have peace with honor as a commitment that America would not abandon them.

John was hopeful that the coming years would open the door to a victory and the end of the war. But there were many more battles to be fought and highs and lows to experience. One thing for sure was that nothing was for sure. Colossians 4:5 was often on his mind: "Redeem the time." There was no time to waste. Along with the sense of urgency he also had a great sense of satisfaction. He was being a good and faithful servant. He had seen Jesus fulfill His promise that "he who is faithful in a very little thing is faithful also in much." He saw the Lord give him ever-increasing responsibilities and fruit for Him. It was an exciting life.

The Lord was also doing great things among the tribes. They were growing in the grace and knowledge of the Lord, many were attending Bible training institutes, and many were sharing their faith. Churches were being established in new places. But God was going to do more. Much more.

Chapter 9

The Revival

Evangelical missionary work through the Christian and Missionary Alliance Church had gone on in Vietnam for many years. Success was measured by the number of converts and established churches among the Vietnamese and the tribal people. It could also be measured by the many programs that were established to meet the various needs of the people. Bible training schools were established to give those who were desirous to serve the Lord a better foundation in church doctrine and hopefully in their personal lives. Success was generally slow but steady, and any missionary would likely feel satisfied with the work that had been done.

All the signs of a growing church were present in the mountain people's churches. People attended services more often than Americans would ever consider. The choir sang better and the special programs were a thrill. The church in the mountains was aflame, but it was soon to experience an explosion. John still sensed that something was missing.

The situation was not unlike many churches of North America at the time. Many churches were experiencing new life after coming out of the hectic days of the sixties, when for a time nothing made sense. Many other churches, however, were cruising along, making some progress, but nothing that would be considered a revival. The pastor of a church in America or Canada would likely be much more aware of the problems that existed in their churches than others in their congregation. They would labor every Sunday to preach that one life-changing sermon that would shake the masses out of their doldrums and lethargy. But every sermon seemed to come up short. There would always be a marginal response, a few smiles, and obligatory congratulations of approval, but people would leave for their homes and only be marginally touched at best.

The tribal church in Vietnam by all outward appearances was much more alive than the churches of North America. In fact, there were many great things to write home about. People in North America who were donating their money could be very satisfied that eternal dividends were being returned on their dollars. The spread of the gospel was dramatically changing lives, and God was being glorified. But if you asked the church leadership and missionaries, they would tell you that they still needed a "revival."

Christians often pray for revival. They sense that spiritual well-being in their church or in their country is lagging behind the will of God. Their hope is that something they do will somehow trigger an outpouring of the Spirit of God. They are not sure what that something is, but they will try it. They will try to have a series of meetings to trigger a revival. They will read about past revivals like the early twentieth-century Welsh revival. They'll have special prayer meetings. They might bring in a special speaker. Often that kind of effort comes short of a true revival. It might spark some conversions, or it might even revive some renewed sense of commitment in many, but ultimately the outpouring of God's Spirit cannot be directed. True revival would come when it would come and where it would come solely by the good pleasure of His will.

True revival came to Vietnam's Central Highlands and to the tribal people in the winter of 1971–72. It is a story of the power of God and the faithfulness of a few. It began from the most unlikely source and probably at the most unlikely time.

The full impact of the American presence in Vietnam was felt by now, and it was not always positive. Most Americans were tired of the war, which seemed endless. Americans felt that their effort to save the South from communism was unappreciated by most of the native people. In the midst of the confusing war and its policy came an American intervention success story that few have ever reported or measured. Its true impact on the country is being felt to this day by thousands of mountain people in Vietnam.

It all started with four American GIs who had recently been converted to Christ through the ministry of Charles Smith of Costa Mesa, California. The soldiers had been shipped to Vietnam but wanted to share their newfound faith. In California the GIs went up and down the beaches witnessing to anybody who would listen. So when they got to Vietnam they wanted to do at least that much. They asked the chaplain of their unit for gospel tracts to hand out to the Vietnamese on the beach next to where they were stationed. They didn't know the language, but they thought maybe this method could reach these war-weary people. They joyously went up and down the beach with contagious grins, handing out the message of eternal life to anyone who would care to read it. They, like many Americans, were confused about their role in Vietnam as soldiers, but they weren't confused about their role as Christians. Their Christian mission was to go to the ends of the earth and make disciples, and since they found themselves all the way on the other side of the globe, they were going to do just that. As they covered that beach and shared what they could, they had the opportunity to share their newfound faith with many Vietnamese.

This so impressed the Vietnamese that word spread about these four, and they were soon invited to speak and give their testimony at the National Bible School in Nha Trang. This Bible school was set up for the entire country of South Vietnam and had about two hundred students, including seven mountain people from the Central Highlands. As they entered the modest one-story school building the students were curious about these young Americans and what they had to say. Of course they had to speak through an interpreter. The brokenness of the presentation of these young, totally-excited-about-Jesus soldiers didn't dilute the impact of the message one bit. The GIs simply told about how they were lost and now were found. More specifically, they shared how they had been delivered from alcohol and drugs to serve the living Savior. They told of how God had convicted them of their sins of dishonesty, lust, selfishness, fornication, and greed.

These young men by virtue of being American were considered by the people of Vietnam as having everything that anyone could possibly want in life. The GIs, however, told how they realized that they really had nothing without Jesus Christ. That when they heard and understood how Christ had come to die and take their sins away so that they could have life eternal, they melted before the Lord and surrendered their lives to Him. The unrestricted joy that they were experiencing from Jesus was pouring forth like a fountain of fresh water onto the students of the school. On that one day the whole school changed.

The students sat in stunned silence. A deep sense of conviction of sin began to take place among the student body. It took everyone by surprise. After all, these were the cream of the crop as far as spirituality was concerned. But the conviction came and there was great confession of sin. These untrained American soldiers simply told their story, and the Holy Spirit used them to speak and penetrate into the souls of these Vietnamese Bible school students. These students began to confess their sins openly to the entire school. They confessed sins of gossiping and lack of love and genuineness, impurity and some of stealing. One after the other, students would get up and confess and repent before the student body, and the whole place would end up in tears. In many ways they were surprised with each other, thinking that so-and-so would never do that. But they soon realized that they all had secret sins. This went on for hours, totally interrupting the school class schedule.

For two weeks during chapel and other times the students confessed and wept and got things right between themselves and the Lord, and also with each other. What took place was a first-class revival (defined as coming back to alertness or awakening) of the National Bible School student body. The Spirit moved individually and corporately through the school, affecting everyone. Everyone associated with the school knew that something unique was happening. The staff was likewise amazed at the transformation going on in the lives of the students. By the end of the term near the Christmas break the place was on fire with renewed and enthusiastic young people anxious to share the reality of Christ in their lives.

The seven students from the mountain tribes were thrilled to go back home to their churches near Da Lat and Ban Me Thuot during the Christmas break and tell the people how wonderfully alive they felt in their relationship with Christ since the last few weeks of the semester had brought revival.

In Da Lat on December 19, 1971, the church had its Christmas program. This was no ordinary Christmas program as seen in North American churches where the little kids get up in front of the church and whisper out a song with a lot of prompting and such. Cute as that might be, the mountain people of Vietnam practiced from October to December for this very important outreach program. Young and old would participate in drama and intricate four-part harmony singing. The program had become one of the major events of the year for the village people. The whole village would come out to see this spectacular performance. Even the littlest ones would carry out their parts flawlessly. The opportunity for evangelism was always great, because many of the non-Christian people would come. The program was a success as usual, and following the program was a reception for the students who had just returned from the National Bible School.

The meeting hall was abuzz with chattering voices full of congratulations. The excitement filling the air was not unlike other years shortly after the Christmas program. After everyone had received their punch and cookies, people began to quiet down as one by one the students gave their expected speeches upon their return. The first student, a girl, approached the front of the crowd. Typically shy, she began to speak of the transforming days at the Bible school just a few days ago. Words came flowing from her mouth, smooth and articulate and full of sincerity that no one could deny. She sensed God speaking through her to the audience as she saw several begin to cry and hang their heads. She continued with her own confession and told how the Lord lifted her up after she finally gave everything over to Jesus. She told how difficult it was to admit to Him who she really was, but when she finally did it was a relief of indescribable proportions. Her speech set the tone for the other students to talk. The intensity grew as each one spoke. Each word spoken confirmed the one previous. It was merely the beginning of what many believe is still going on to this very day in the mountains of Central Vietnam.

The students simply gave their testimony about how they had heard the reality of Christ in their lives from those four American soldiers and how it brought deep conviction of sin. They told how it was like hearing the gospel for the first time and how the Lord spoke to each of them deep in their hearts. The words they said were once again "delicious on our ears." They told how they had so often been phony in their previous testimonies and singing engagements. Now they weren't phony. This was real. As each one continued with a similar story it rang a true chord in the hearts of many of the young people who were present. They began to identify intensely with the Bible school students, thinking they too were often hypocritical in their Christian walk.

Scores of young people present began to feel that same powerful conviction the students had felt just a couple of weeks earlier. Many who had been dragging their feet in their commitment to the Lord cried out loud and confessed their sluggishness of heart and the sins that were entangling them. As more and more testified to the same conviction, more and more were overwhelmed. The meeting was like no other before.

Many testified that they had received Christ as their Savior only for extra protection from the bullets or other accidents; they kept a Cambodian charm with them just in case. This "just in case" approach to their Christian walk was what was getting in the way of them having a meaningful relationship with Christ. Others confessed to sexual sins, petty theft, or backstabbing. Whatever their sin, the people felt the presence of the Lord so strongly that they could not ignore it. He was there with them and there was no denying it. What was happening to others as well as to themselves was a real work of God's Spirit bringing them closer to Him.

What happened at the Christmas reception was exactly what happened at the National Bible School and very similar to what happened at Simpson College in Seattle when John was attending school—an overwhelming outpouring of God's Spirit that had never been experienced before in that place. The meeting began at 11 p.m. and lasted until 4 a.m. the next morning. By four o'clock they had gotten it all out.

Those who weren't yet Christians came to the Lord that night after seeing the reality of Christ in the lives of their peers. The hours seemed like seconds. People both young and old were elated and exhausted at the same time.

John said it was like "someone throwing gasoline on the crowd and lighting a match; I've never seen anything like it." John, like the other missionaries in the area, was caught off guard and struck with amazement at what he was seeing. It was beyond anything they could conjure up with some kind of program or extended effort. No strategy for success could accomplish what they witnessed take place in just a few hours. Not even a fervent prayer meeting could bring about the deep conviction, confession, and recommitment or salvation that had just taken place on that one evening. It was described and still is described as a merciful, sovereign act on the part of God's Spirit toward the modest people of the Central Highlands of Vietnam. They didn't necessarily ask for it or deserve it, but it happened anyway. And that was only the beginning.

The young evangelists began to hold more meetings, as many as they felt were needed. Each night would be a continuation of the first, one building upon the other in momentum. People of all ages were coming to see what had happened to all the people who had experienced the Lord. They would come to glorify God and to see what might come next. A thirst they didn't even know they had was being satisfied with wells of Living Water. What the mountain people were seeing take place and feeling in their souls was not the result of positive mental activity or that of spirits; it could only be explained in terms of being from the Creator of all life and the Savior of mankind.

John was witness to these things but sensed the Lord would have the missionaries step aside and let the Holy Spirit direct the affairs through the tribespeople themselves. As the momentum built from day to day it became obvious that the missionaries were to play a minor role in all this. In reality this is the missionary's greatest hope: for laypeople to become the evangelists, pastors, and teachers to their own people. All the missionaries were excited about how the Lord Jesus was making Himself real and personal to the needy people of the mountains.

Up high in the cool mountains of Central Vietnam a special warmth was moving through the villages. The village where the first testimonies were given began to send out groups in order to reach the surrounding tribes and villages. These teams would come at any time of the day and set up a meeting. No matter what the people were doing they would come. Rumors of the great outpouring of God's Spirit were already making it to them. They wanted to see for themselves. They were not disappointed. At one church John remembers the singing being so loud, and the obvious excitement of the people made the building rattle. Two tribal soldiers were guarding the church at the time. They became interested in what was going on inside and looked through the windows. Each tine they stuck their heads inside the church they felt the presence of the Lord, and when they were outside they didn't. They knew that the Lord was in the church, so they went inside and asked if they could know this "Jesus" as their Savior too.

The young evangelists would sing with a renewed sense of inspiration, and the preachers would preach with a new sense of confidence and authority. Even when the language was not fully correct the listeners miraculously understood the message. They expanded their outreach to tribes and villages with whom they were less familiar. They intentionally tried to spread the revival to the Ban Me Thuot region among the Rade people.

John and his team were forced to speak only in the Koho language even though the people might not understand most of it. It was all he and others knew, but they would preach the message of salvation anyway, and the people would begin to weep. Somehow, though the people didn't understand the language they understood the message. John said it was not speaking in tongues, but the effect was probably similar. It was definitely a miracle from God. The experience might have been like that of the apostle Paul when he entered a new region.

The people whom God was speaking to would weep bitterly and come forward to receive Jesus as their Savior. Dozens came forward nightly. They somehow knew that they were sinners and in need of the Savior. They knew that the Savior could only be Jesus Christ and none other. The words were not from their language, but something happened between the mouths of the preachers and the ears of the people. Those who know the power of God would call it a miracle. Scoffers would call it group psychological pressure. But all present would know it was from the Lord, that there was no other reasonable explanation. And besides, the presence of the Lord was deeply felt by all.

These mountain people were from a culture that sacrificed animals to appease the spirits. They miraculously heard the words in their own language and understood in their hearts the message even though the speakers were not using their language. They understood the One whose blood sacrifice could alone atone for their failings. They realized they had offended the Creator of all by worshipping the creature instead. Unlike their own sacrifices of chickens, pigs, or water buffalo, this Jesus sacrificed Himself once for them all. No other sacrifice would ever need to be given. What good news this was to a people who would often spend their life savings to sacrifice to the spirits.

The fruit of the revival is still going on today in many ways in the Central Highlands. Over a two-year period between 1971 and 1972 there were twenty-three thousand new believers who turned their lives over to Christ, twenty-three thousand people who turned from a life of demon worship, thieving, lying, and any other imaginable sin. Scores reported healings and deliverance from demon harassment and possession.

John was a part of at least two healings himself. John's theological upbringing didn't emphasize the possibility of miraculous manifestations of the power of God. But they happened without prompting and much fanfare in the mountains of Vietnam in the winter and spring of 1972. The miracles didn't require a special preacher warming up the crowd; they were simply the result of the people's childlike faith and the pure mercy of the Holy Spirit.

In one such case John was asked to pray for an old non-Christian man. The man was suffering from an illness that could easily have taken his life. The family had tried everything they knew, including some of their spirit worship and making sacrifices. They were desperate and running out of choices. The village people figured the "white" missionary could probably do something to help. So John was called to the village chieftain's home. He was a bit hesitant because he was afraid the Lord might choose to allow the sickness to continue. But these were unusual times, and the Lord was doing amazing things for His glory. So he decided to go and trust the Lord for whatever might happen through him.

It was an evening in the early spring of 1972. The revival had been going on for several months, and even the most skeptical tribesman was realizing that something very amazing was happening to the Christian people. John carefully climbed up the longhouse steps into the familiar smoky room. He was breathing a quick silent prayer for divine assistance as he stood to see where the ill man lay.

John, having been put on the spot, prayed in Koho and asked God to have mercy and heal this man for His glory. It was a short, simple prayer. It was a mustard seed of faith. The man was instantaneously healed. It about knocked

John off his feet. He had prayed a thousand healing prayers before and seen God answer many of them, but never had there been such instant response. John was as surprised as the unsaved tribal people that surrounded him. Upon seeing this outpouring of God, the village people wanted to know more of this Jesus. John gladly shared the simple gospel with them, and many came to know the Savior that night.

In another case, John was asked to go to the longhouse of another village chief. His little granddaughter was gravely ill. Everyone tried to do something for her, but nothing would help. The flicker of life was going out of her, and everyone around knew she would be dead soon if something didn't happen. Though they weren't believers, out of desperation they asked the missionaries for some help. They had heard about the great things the white man's God had done, and they wanted His help now.

When John got to the longhouse it was rapidly approaching evening. A slight coolness to the air was beginning to descend on the village. He stepped up the ladder and into the longhouse, which was the home of several families. The fire gave some light to the room, but smoke filled the air and made the room a haze. Many people had gathered around the fire and the child. There was a lot of chatter and expectation. They were all sitting cross-legged, and the village chief's granddaughter lay near the fire, small, fragile, weak, and barely conscious. The chief was desperate and anxious for any kind of help.

Death was not uncommon to these people, but love for a child is universal. All eyes were on John as he sat down cross-legged, not sure what he was going to do. All of the people quickly became quiet, though skeptical, in anticipation of John's coming prayer.

John was sitting there in near panic because he had once again been put on the spot. He had recently seen God work mightily in the case of the old man. He knew God was working something special here in the mountains, so his confidence was beginning to grow. But this was uncharted territory for John. So he prayed in Koho, "Look, Lord, we are on the spot here; have mercy on this child for Your name's sake, amen." Another missionary present prayed in Vietnamese. They had tried to feed the child for days and she couldn't hold any food down. After the prayers she seemed a little bit better. They gave the child some rice gruel, and she took it and started to revive immediately. The little girl had been healed by the power of the God of the missionary. As a result of that evidence, the chieftain asked to hear more of this God. John had the opportunity to share the gospel with him and everyone present. Thirty-five people were added to the Kingdom that night and began to attend church.

The ripples from the revival were having amazing effects throughout the Central Highlands. As more came to a saving knowledge of Christ they enthusiastically brought with them their family and friends. They saw and felt the reality of the risen Lord. Tribal people were exercising simple, childlike faith and seeing Him do wonders.

One such wonder came that spring at a village near Ban Me Thuot. A 16-year-old boy had died from an illness. As eyewitnesses reported it, the boy's body had become cold and stiff and was ready for burial, and the family was near it, weeping their loss. The village men built a crude coffin to prepare him for burial. With so many wonderful things the Lord was doing in the mountains the reality of death, sickness, and war were still all around.

One of the new converts to Christ had read about Jesus healing the sick and even raising the dead. He hadn't been trained in Bible school, nor did he have all the church doctrines down pat, but he had faith. It was true childlike faith in the power of God. Perhaps only faith the size of a tiny mustard seed, but he believed in the power of the Lord. He began to pray along with some other fellow believers.

The family was weeping as they laid the boy in the box and prepared him for burial. The young believers began to pray over his body in the name of the Lord before they closed the coffin. As they prayed earnestly, to their utter astonishment, warmth and color began to return to the body. It seemed impossible, but it was happening. His eyes began to twitch, and he suddenly opened them and the boy was revived. Risen.

The astonishment of those present was indescribable. The breathtaking event that took place before their eyes was incomprehensible but also undeniable. They had witnessed the most amazing manifestation of the power of God known to man. John did not witness this event, but it was confirmed by scores of credible witnesses among the tribal people.

Word spread about the raising-the-dead incident in the village area. It served to open the minds of the most doubtful to the claims of Jesus Christ. After all, they had a living witness to a miracle of God's grace right before their eyes. The Christian leaders estimate that six hundred people came to put their trust in Jesus as a result of the boy being raised. John felt it must have been very much like the days described in Acts 2:47: "The Lord was adding to their number day by day those who were being saved."

Sau A, along with Uncle Kar, went to the Mekong River Delta region to witness to the Vietnamese people what God was doing in the Central Highlands. The excitement of the mountain people seeing the work of God could not be contained. They wanted to tell anyone who would listen to the gospel of Jesus as they had, and they hoped that others would experience the power of His salvation.

The Vietnamese and mountain people never had gotten along and had little respect for one another. However, this time hundreds of Vietnamese came to hear their testimony. That in itself was a miracle. As Sau A and Uncle Kar delivered their stories of Jesus Christ working among the tribes in a mighty way, great emotion poured forth from them. The Vietnamese sat in stunned silence. They had never felt the presence of the Lord like this in their entire lives. They had never seen such true joy and conviction of spirit. The hundreds who were present came under great spiritual conviction of their need for Christ as their own personal Savior and Lord. Scores gave their life to Christ that day, and even more Christians rededicated their lives to Him.

This is what those days were like all throughout the Central Highlands, and beyond in some cases. It was a time when God chose to move among a people and change their lives from the inside out. Tribal folks leading tribal folks to the Lord, using languages that hadn't even been written. All this was started by some enthusiastic American GIs. These four men probably don't even know what they started. They were simply faithful to obey His command at that moment in time. Their faithfulness spread to thousands of others in exponential growth. The amazing fact is that the harvest continues to this day. There were about 35,000 Christians in the Central Highlands before Christmas of 1971, and now there are an estimated 94,000 believers among the Koho-speaking people alone, most as a direct and ongoing result of the revival that began in December of 1971.

Chapter 10

Darkness Falls over the Land of Vietnam

President Richard Nixon, through the diplomatic skills of Henry Kissinger, was able to negotiate the end of American ground and air involvement in Vietnam in the spring of 1973. An Easter NVA offensive to overrun the South had ultimately failed. This settlement was a compromise agreement toward the peace with honor the president had been seeking throughout his tenure. It was also a compromise for the North, seeing as they had no obvious military victory. It was, however, a cease-fire and a way for the U.S. to appear to have achieved its objective of stopping communist advancement. Few with any political savvy would be fooled into thinking that this would secure South Vietnam's freedom.

Over the years between 1972 to 1975 leading up to the fall of South Vietnam, the tribal people continued to enjoy the ongoing fruits of the revival. More and more people came to Christ as teams of young people hit the ragged roads and steep trails to reach their fellow mountain tribes.

John was tireless in those days. The energy of the kids around him inspired him to make all the arrangements needed to by evangelistic teams. Basic details such as keeping the

Land Rover up and running and filled with gas were on his shoulders. They would load up the Land Rover with guitars and with kids ready to sing and share their testimonies to the next village. It was a time of great excitement. John would rarely preach, because the young Christians would preach more effectively and see many come forward. The young people, as they gave their testimonies and shared the Word of God, would sense the power of the Holy Spirit. As in the early days of the revival, occasional healings were reported and broken relationships were repaired, and marginally committed believers were openly confessing their sins.

The pressure to seize the time for evangelism in Vietnam did not change much in these months of relative peace. Upon signing the peace accord the North Vietnamese, South Vietnamese, and United States had specific provisions of the agreement that each were to follow. The United States was required to withdraw all troops upon exchange of POWs. The agreement prohibited the North and U.S. from sending any more troops into South Vietnam. It also provided for what essentially was a coalition government made up of the existing leadership of the South Vietnamese; the National Liberation Front, or Vietcong, as most knew them; and some other interest groups. Four years of sluggish negotiations that began in the fall of 1968 ended in a flawed agreement that would eventually leave the door wide open to an invasion that was met with little resistance.

The North Vietnamese already had 219,000 troops in the South at the signing. Within the first two weeks the North had committed over two hundred major violations of the accords. Among those violations was the infiltration of 75,000 troops into South Vietnam and increasing its tank strength from 100 to 500. The U.S., knowing of these violations, chose to ignore them. This only served to underscore the great vulnerability of the South to eventual all-out attack.

The North determined that the United States would not take any significant action to stop an all-out offensive. Nixon was embroiled in the Watergate scandal, and Americans simply wanted to put Vietnam behind them. In December 1974 fighting was taking place in Phuoc Luong northeast of Saigon. The U.S. did not respond, so the North began plans for an offensive for the spring of 1975.

John and Jo enjoyed some of the most fruitful times of their ministry in the months following the peace agreement. As things began to settle down a bit, the new converts from the '72 revival were growing in the Lord. More students were attending Bible school, and more were involved in evangelistic teams.

In the spring of 1975 there were rumblings of a new offensive. The South Vietnamese army was well equipped and manned, but they were set up in a defensive posture. This always gives the enemy an upper hand. They can better observe your weaknesses and strike whenever they want.

It was difficult to tell whether this new buildup was a serious crisis. John and Jo had endured crisis after crisis in the country they had grown to love. However, the U.S. government perceived it as serious and gave a warning to all American personnel in Vietnam. The warning given to all U.S. missionaries and personnel was to pack their drums (large industrial drums were used by most missionaries to transport their belongings to the field) and report to the nearest airport and prepare to evacuate. It had the definite ring of crisis, but was met with sort of a "cry wolf" reaction. However, it soon became clear that this was no overreaction or false warning.

The North Vietnamese began to push south from the northern regions of South Vietnam, starting near the demilitarized zone (DMZ) at the 17th parallel. This assault was the closest to conventional war tactics used by the North Vietnamese in the whole war. They brazenly took city after city in a sweep that surprised even the experts. Familiar places like Kai San and Hue were quickly lost, and a retreat of the SVN army was taking place.

Jo Newman went on to Nha Trang as quickly as she could find a ride. She and several other wives got in a station wagon and evacuated from Da Lat. The missionary men stayed in Da Lat. Because the full weight of the crisis was not yet apparent, John went south to Saigon for a quick trip. It seemed at first that this was just another false alarm. John needed do some banking, so he went to Saigon to get money and supplies, fully expecting to return and weather this current storm. Besides getting the necessary funds for operating the mission base, John was looking forward to his customary purchase of some pomelo fruit to hand out to fellow missionaries on his way home to Da Lat. However, while he was in Saigon, the communist forces came too close to the city of Da Lat. The U.S. Embassy revised its earlier request and ordered all U.S. personnel out of Da Lat by morning. John was at a loss as to what to do. He couldn't get back to Da Lat, and Jo was in Nha Trang with no way to communicate with her. He assumed she was safe, but there was no way to know for sure. If this was the end, then all of their possessions short of what Jo had packed would be lost. He would have to wait and pray. They were agonizing hours.

Back in Da Lat, the clinic that John had established was in a mad dash to pack up their goods and get out of the region. The clinic had to let the patients who were in bed go back to their homes without any further care. Two doctors and four nurses hurriedly packed as many hospital supplies as possible into their drums. Then the U.S. Embassy provincial senior advisor called the missionaries. They were to be ready to evacuate by 8 a.m. the next morning.

This was hardly enough time to make all the necessary preparations. It was apparent now that to escape with their lives would be all that they could hope for. Seven vehicles loaded with missionaries from the area took off early that April morning to get out with their lives. The caravan included the doctors and nurses of the clinic, teachers at the language school in Da Lat, Catholic nuns and priests who had studied at the school, and the area's evangelical missionaries. They wanted to drive as a caravan down to Saigon, but the communists had already cut off the road. They decided their only option was to drive to Nha Trang.

The caravan first had to travel down to Phan Rang, then up Highway 1 to Nha Trang. They got to the airport and USAID flew them all out that evening to Saigon. John was frantic as he had heard how critical things were at the home base. It was clear to him by now that travel back to Da Lat was impossible. He could only hope that Jo would not get caught in between messages of evacuation and head somewhere that was dangerous. He hoped and prayed that they would meet up soon by God's grace.

"If this is the beginning of the end," John thought, "the tribal people are in for a terrible time." Since the tribal people had consistently supported the U.S. and SVN over the years, a fierce revenge might be in store at the hands of the North Vietnamese and Vietcong. The mountain people had decided to continue the fight against the communists, but the newly reinforced NVA had come with tanks this time. The long-standing hatred of the Vietnamese came out in full-blown expression when the mountain people were overwhelmed by the unfamiliar tanks (they were used to smaller-scale, more guerrilla-type warfare in the mountains). As village people near Ban Me Thuot were running for their lives through a rubber plantation, NVA tanks opened fire and mercilessly mowed them down with their machine guns and ran over their bodies. A camera was present at the massacre and filmed the whole grisly event, and it was shown on Western news channels. The deep-set indifference of the American people to the affairs of Vietnam sparked no emotion or outcry. Hundreds lost their lives. This event in Ban Me Thuot was only a fore-shadowing of tragedies yet to come.

The people living in the southern sector of South Vietnam were rapidly getting the impression that this might be the end for them as a country. The communist forces were rapidly moving systematically down the country like no other time in the history of the war. The days took on a strange and eerie tone as impending doom was approaching.

John had heard that a USAID plane was coming in from Nha Trang with evacuated missionaries. He knew that Jo was supposed to be on that plane, but he prayed just the same. The Newmans were successfully reunited at the airport in Saigon. Their meeting was a combination of desperate antic-ipation and indescribable relief. They knew this might be the final hour. All the missionaries who came down from the Da Lat region were housed temporarily at the World Vision guesthouse in Saigon.

Those days were agonizing, sitting cramped together in the guesthouse, unable to do anything or communicate with the people they loved and had worked with for nineteen years, knowing that these might be their last days in the country. Difficult thoughts flooded John's mind, knowing that they might never see again their beloved brothers and sisters in the Lord from the Rade, Koho, and Monong people. The innocent, smiling faces of the children might never be seen again. Having to leave their home without being able to take anything short of what they could carry left an indescribable emptiness.

There had always been the knowledge that this day would come. The hope of any positive turn in events was rapidly fading. The U.S. would not come and save the day. They had made that clear months earlier when the peace accord violations were less severe. As the agonizing days went on, everyone made desperate attempts to put critical matters in order, sometimes successfully and sometimes not.

Within days it became clear that simply getting out of the country alive would be an act of mercy. Leaving the land they loved and the people that had drawn close to their hearts over the years was almost too much to bear. Jo was so overcome with grief that she began to experience symptoms of nervous exhaustion, breaking out in hives and showing signs of depression. John kept a stiff upper lip as he tried to get some of his tribal people out during the evacuation. He knew the communist forces would attempt to retaliate against them. Fear of a bloodbath was becoming all too real, especially after seeing what happened in Ban Me Thuot.

Always strong in the midst of a crisis, John's concern turned to getting themselves and his fellow missionaries out of the country as soon as possible. His concern was not only for his own safety; he wondered if he could manage to get some of his closest tribal friends out too. He would pull any strings possible to get them out. He had many connections with the Army, Air Force, USAID, and the South Vietnamese government. He was going to use any of these and more if possible to get some of his tribal friends out. It would literally mean he could be saving their lives if successful.

As a matter of U.S. Embassy policy, priority was given to all American personnel to be lifted out of the country first. Second priority would be key South Vietnamese officials. The last in line for emergency evacuation would be any tribal people. This gave little hope for any mountain people getting a chance to leave. It would take nothing short of a miracle. Time was running out rapidly for the first-priority group, let alone the second. No official was going to go out on a limb for a handful of tribal people when it meant taking the place of some Vietnamese. With all these factors against them, it didn't deter John's hope. So he immediately sought to get some of them down to Saigon any way possible without getting killed.

John was able to get four young tribesmen to journey to Saigon in the middle of the heavy fighting. Four tribal girls were already in Saigon attending school. It was by the grace of God that the young men were not captured along the way, because the road they traveled was quickly falling into enemy hands. In all, there was the possibility of getting eight tribal people out of Vietnam. There were two Rade men and six Koho; Ha Jimmy and Ha Johnny were among them. However, they were not planning on leaving Vietnam when they came. They were determined to stay and fight if necessary. Jimmy was in the military and had just been promoted in the last days of the war.

Comprehension of what was actually taking place hadn't fully set in yet. But as soon as the situation in South Vietnam became hopeless they quickly made arrangements to leave the country. There was hardly any time for them to think. They would not be able to go back to their villages and say goodbye or gather precious belongings. They would be leaving their home soon, likely never to return. Never to see their families or their brothers and sisters in the Lord again in this lifetime. It was heartrending. They hadn't prepared mentally for this change that was being forced on them. They knew that if they wanted to live they would have to leave. Their hearts were heavy with the reality of having to evacuate and leave their brothers and sisters in Christ forever.

John and Jo got their own papers in order and bought commercial flight tickets to Hong Kong, where they would meet up with the other missionaries. It was still hard to believe that this was the end. But there was no mistaking that fact. As they would sit for hours awaiting the next step in their escape, the big artillery guns could be heard in the distance. Smoke from the exploding artillery shells hung over the sweltering city like a cloud of impending doom.

Amazingly, many people in Saigon went on with their daily business like there was little concern.

John recalls having to walk through the American Embassy and adjoining courtyard to get to the World Vision guesthouse and out of the country the night before the last day of freedom in South Vietnam. What was going on at the embassy was difficult to comprehend. American personnel at the embassy, along with some military brass, had arranged for a huge party. The party had a band playing dance tunes, and the place was filled with elaborate decorations. The smell of smoke from the approaching artillery and the crack of gunfire were being ignored, as was any sense of impropriety on the part of those participating. The men had their "girlfriends," and there was excessive drinking and revelry. The missionaries who were walking through this scene were appalled at the chosen blindness on the part of these Americans.

The scene seemed to be representative of American involvement in Vietnam. In many ways the Americans brought good and the possibility for good. But in other ways they brought out the worst in the people because of the massive amount of American dollars that were so alluring and corruptive. The American presence was a mixed blessing at best. It did, however, give people like the Newmans about ten extra years to get the good news of Jesus to the people. As a result, hundreds came to faith in Jesus Christ and received eternal life. However, the door was about to be shut. The future was dim. It seemed the light was rapidly going out.

That night they made their flight to Hong Kong. Within hours the scene at the embassy would change from gaiety to desperate attempts to lift people from the rooftop of the building by helicopter. Before they left, John was making every effort possible to see that the eight young tribal people could get out of the country safely. Jimmy got hold of a military jeep and took some missionaries to the Tan Son Nhat

Airport. He dropped them off and was anxious to get back to his fellow tribal soldier. He was extremely worried they might be overcome by the communists at any moment. After he dropped off the missionaries at the airport he attempted to return to the city and perhaps make his way back to the Da Lat region. SVN soldiers would not let him go back, because the enemy was already inside the city.

It turned out that this was providential for Jimmy. He no doubt would have been killed if he had returned. He was famous among the communist forces as the leader of the Montagnard resistance and for having cooperated with American intelligence. Almost anyone connected with such overt assistance with the Americans faced certain death or imprisonment.

With hundreds of Vietnamese nationals seeking a way out, the miracle of getting the lowly mountain people out safely was about to occur. John had been able to convince the people at USAID to grant them space on their airplane. The plane, packed as full as was possible, was the last to leave and transported its human cargo to Clark Air Base in the Philippines. The eight tribal people who made it out of Vietnam with the help of John and others were the only tribal people in the whole country to escape.

John and Jo met up with their fellow missionaries in Hong Kong. They checked into their hotel, still in shock at what had just transpired. Everything seemed to be in slow motion, yet dramatic events were taking place at breakneck speed. The whole experience was almost overwhelming. It seemed to John and Jo that it was just days ago that they were living in peace in the cool mountains of Da Lat.

Money was graciously made available to them in these days of crisis through the Billy Graham Association. This organization often gave thousands of dollars to causes that rarely would receive any attention. This was a major blessing to many of the evacuated missionaries because of the circumstances of being forced to leave. Some were not able to get all of their money out of the banks, and some just didn't have the emergency resources for such a time.

That evening the missionaries all had dinner together at one of the hotels. It was a strange meal. Under normal circumstances it would be a delight to be eating together in a Hong Kong hotel. But this was no ordinary moment. This was a gathering of people who had just escaped with their lives. Who had left their lifelong work and dearest friends in an instant. The shock of what had just happened to them had not yet penetrated their stunned minds. The conversation ranged from shallow small talk to stories of escape. The realization that life would never be the same from that moment on was almost too much to bear. But all would attest to God's unfailing love and grace. They were shocked, stunned, and hurt, but their faith remained. Their love for the people remained. But it was over.

They watched on television (along with every American alive at the time) the final helicopter lifting off the American Embassy roof having to push people away. They saw the crowds of people clambering at the walls and gates of the embassy, hoping for a slim chance of escape. They knew how each of those people seeking escape felt. They witnessed the aircraft carrier deck full of refugees pushing a multimillion-dollar helicopter into the South China Sea like it were an old piece of furniture, just to make room. They knew that untold horrors awaited those left behind, especially the professional people and anyone known to have helped the Americans. Then, in silence they watched tanks rolling down the Saigon avenues with their big red star on the side of the turret and waving the communist flag. The curtain had fallen.

John and Jo flew on from Hong Kong to Bangkok, Thailand, along with their longtime friends and fellow Overseas Crusades missionaries from Beacon Chapel in Spokane, Glenn and Hallie Johnson. They stayed in Bangkok a few days and then were airlifted to Guam. The tribal people were flown from Clark Air Base to Guam, and the Newmans were able to meet up with them there. From there they all flew to Hawaii for a stop, and then on to California. This all took place in just a few hours.

The refugees—American, tribal, and Vietnamese—were mostly in a state of confusion and shock. They were all grateful, however, to have the chance to go to America, the land of great wealth, beauty, and opportunity. But they were leaving their home, their families, and their friends, and heartache filled each one. Their first stop in America took place in the evening. It was a dreary journey into the unknown for the refugees. They unloaded from the airplane and boarded buses to a place called Camp Pendleton, which is only few miles north of San Diego.

They all arrived at Camp Pendleton at 3 a.m. It was cold, dark, and raining. The soldiers handed out three blankets for everyone, and they were shown to their sleeping quarters. When light came that morning the refugees could not believe their eyes. This was nothing like they had imagined America to be. The low, rolling terrain hugging the coastline of the Pacific was nothing but yellowish-brown grass as far as the eye could see. "Where is the green?" everyone thought. These people were used to rich greens everywhere, and now they were in a desolate desert. "This couldn't be America," many of them thought. If there was any hope for a fantasy-fulfilled life in America, it was dissipating rapidly into a sea of homesickness and disappointment. This was the experience of nearly all of the 48,000 Vietnamese.

American officials were caught off guard by this enormous influx of people. They were forced to make quick and life-affecting decisions in a very short period of time. The refugees were helpless. They were completely at the mercy of the American officials. The officials were scarcely able to house and feed the people, let alone make arrangements for official entry into the country with papers. John and Jo wanted to get off the base and were able to secure a motel room nearby. They were in great need of physical and emotional rest, but the work had just begun. There was no time for relaxing or taking some sort of holiday to recuperate from the ordeal. Now they needed to figure out a way to get the mountain people out of Camp Pendleton. Getting them out of the chaotic setting of the camp would be the best way to help them on to a new life somewhere in America.

This was particularly difficult because John and Jo were facing their own uncertainty as well. It required a selfless attitude. John recalls the special grace and energy of the Holy Spirit during those days for himself, but sadly, Jo continued to show signs of exhaustion and depression. John was caught in two crises now: taking adequate care of his suffering wife and working on behalf of his people. He was particularly afraid the tribal people might get lost in the shuffle. Jo showed some positive signs and encouraged John to do what he could for the tribal "kids." She knew that soon the day was coming when they would be back in Spokane to rest and recover both physically and emotionally.

John and Steve Wilcox of World Relief Commission worked for a month at Camp Pendleton to get refugees out of the camp and relocated. They alone managed to get nine hundred refugees out and sent to Camp Hope (named after Bob Hope), where World Vision provided food and other relief services. From there they were able to better process the refugees and begin placing them in communities around the country, and set up needed services and jobs for them so they could get their new lives started.

The days were filled with a whirlwind of contrary emotions for everyone. Truly it was the death of an old life and the beginning of a new life for so many. Not knowing the wheres, whens, hows, and most of all the whys made it nearly unbearable at times. This is when a true and living faith came into play. The Lord of all, the only Sovereign, could still be trusted. Those exhausting days finally came to an end for John and Jo when they were able to get their tribal kids released from the camp and into their personal care. The Newmans quickly headed for their daughter's comfortable home in Spokane for some much-needed rest. It was June 1975.

With the fall of South Vietnam, there was heavy interest among the American Christian community concerning the stories of escape and spiritual opportunity. John, barely taking a breather upon returning to the States, quickly set up a meeting in the Spokane Opera House to let the tribal refugees speak and witness to the grace of God in their lives through their ordeal. Jimmy and Johnny were the best spokesmen. Hundreds were encouraged by how the two were still praising God in the midst of their loss, and some came to the Lord upon hearing their testimony. They had other speaking engagements around the Northwest in the weeks during that summer. But soon the dust began to settle and the true sorrow of what had taken place began to settle in.

Those nagging, unanswered questions began to flood in as the days of rest and recuperation were finally allowed to begin. John could not continue to meet the demand for speaking engagements, and he too slowed down. The rush of events over the past three months was met with many "why" questions for John. Why didn't the Americans keep their commitment to South Vietnam, why did they sign such a flawed peace accord, why was the South Vietnamese government so corrupt and unprepared to defend their country, why did the politicians continually frustrate the war effort, why did so many Americans protest the war, why, why, why?

John's perspective was part political, part spiritual. He wrestled with this constantly, with no chance for clear resolution. There seemed to be several realities to the war. What he saw was only a portion of reality. One perspective was that of the missionaries, who saw any effort to keep the communists out as ultimately helpful because the work of the gospel could continue. Another was that of the American military, which never seemed to be able to fight the war without some kind of restraint, and a third was that of the American public which was developed by the information provided through various media sources. The perspective that prevailed was that of the American public. The U.S. had lost its altruism for the Vietnamese cause a long time before the spring of 1975.

As the communists began to take hold of the South, changes were rapidly taking place, representative of the new era. Saigon, the city designed by the French to mirror Paris, the city where the good and evil of capitalism were apparent everywhere, had its name changed to Ho Chi Minh City. The celebration in the streets had rapidly digressed into persecution and oppression unimaginable. Everyone in Vietnam who had any official government position, or were known collaborators with the Americans, or were professional people had to scramble to seek some new identity or cover their past somehow. Executions were common. Forced labor and imprisonment were common. Possessions were being looted everywhere. No one was safe.

The country had been reduced to a horror story. The tribes of the Central Highlands were particularly vulnerable. Their horrors were double those of the Vietnamese nationals. They were actively being pursued by the communist forces, who had revenge on their mind. The mountain people were hunted like animals in the mountains as far as Laos and Cambodia. Particularly at risk of harm were Christian leaders and pastors. The communists saw the pastors as those most responsible for anticommunist sentiments. This scenario would set the stage for a new crisis, and John's heart for the people of Vietnam would not allow him to sit back and do nothing.

Chapter 11

Rescue the Perishing

The years following the fall of Vietnam were a time of uncertainty for John and Jo. They kept in contact with the handful of tribal people they had managed to get out of the country. Ha Johnny was working in Spokane at a lumber supply company. Ha Jimmy was traveling around the country speaking about the needs of the people of his country and testifying to the Lord's grace in getting them out of Vietnam just in the nick of time.

John was restless in the months after the fall of Vietnam. Though he never slipped into anything one would consider depression, he was very discouraged by the events that led to them being forced to leave Vietnam. He had poured his life out for this ministry, and now it was suddenly gone. He loved those people with all his heart, and he knew life would be difficult for most of them and many of his closest friends would be killed with the communists in control. He wanted to do something, but there was nothing he could do. All he could do was pray.

This whole ordeal brought Jo to a point of exhaustion. As she and John settled into their daughter's home in Spokane, she slowly rehabilitated, but it took months. The physical and most of all the emotional strain were almost too much.

They both hung on to every encouraging word from the Bible they could. It often took every ounce of faith they had. They had just been forced to leave their work, their brothers and sisters in Christ, and the land they had grown to love with all their hearts. It hurt like no other hurt they had experienced in their lives. They held on for dear life to the words of Isaiah 40:31:

Those who wait for the LORD will gain new
    strength;
They will mount up with wings like eagles,
They will run and not get tired,
They will walk and not become weary.

Though this didn't happen in an instant, over time the Lord gave them both that strength. The Lord sustained both of them and brought them both to a point where their energy was restored, but it did take several months. Their vision to serve Him was revived, and they sought the Lord's will for their lives.

John had no specific ministry after the fall of Vietnam and wondered what kind of usefulness he and Jo could have in the future. Though he was at retirement age he wanted his later years to count for some eternal good. He didn't want to sit around and let someone else do what he knew he could do. So John did whatever he could. He served as guest speaker at many missions conferences around the region and would preach in churches from time to time. John didn't want to waste a minute. The world was rapidly spinning out of control, as it had for decades, and John still had that sense of evangelical urgency. But this was a time for waiting on God. Waiting for direction. It was one of the most difficult times of his life. He simply wanted to make an impact on human lives for eternity. It made sense to him that he be used to help the people of Vietnam, since he had so much training and experience there. But that door was now closed.

As God would have it, there would be no retirement for John, and he would even have a chance to serve the people of Vietnam. As the months turned to years, a new tragedy in Southeast Asia was unfolding. John had become deeply concerned about the reports coming out of Vietnam that up to 90 percent of those attempting to leave the country by boat were dying at sea. The "boat people," as they were called, were fleeing the unbearable oppression of communist rule in Vietnam.

The reunification of Vietnam meant many changes for the South. "Reeducation camps" were set up to indoctrinate the people about the evils of capitalism. A person couldn't even have a small vegetable garden under their strict regulations. In order to get the South Vietnamese to fully understand and embrace the new communist regime, they forced thousands to endure these camps. The law of the land was for all to serve the needs of the state. Anything less than that would be seen as treason and worthy of severe punishment. At the camps, beatings, murder, malnourishment, and psychological cruelties were commonplace. Though the communists condemned the evils of selfishness, their selfish ambition far exceeded that of their subjects. This indoctrination was pursued with a cultish, evangelical fervor. Darkness was over the entire land of Vietnam. The light of hope had been turned off by the oppressive and antireligious ideology of communism. As this became clearer to the people of Vietnam, they began to take steps to escape the clutches of communist oppression by sacrificing everything to leave the country.

John's deep concern could not let him sit back and watch more and more people perish. Even as he approached 70 years old he would soon find himself back in Asia laboring to save people from certain destruction. He would soon be fulfilling the lyrics of one of his favorite missionary hymns:

Rescue the perishing, care for the dying,
Snatch them in pity from sin and the grave;
Weep o'er the erring one, lift up the fallen,
Tell them of Jesus, the mighty to save.

He would do this by pulling starving, desperate souls from the dangerous waters of the South China Sea.

All the fears of the past two decades were coming to pass with the communist regime in Vietnam. Thousands of Vietnamese were imprisoned, killed, or forced out of work. The mountain people of the Central Highlands were actively being hunted because of their strong support of the United States during the war. The tribes had to escape deeper into the mountains, as far as Cambodia in many cases. Mere survival was almost impossible for the tribal people, but they managed with ingenuity and courage.

Pastor Sau A, Jimmy and Johnny's father and the spiritual father of hundreds of mountain people, survived courageously for three years, but was killed by the communists in 1978. After hiding out in the mountains in small bands, his group was found and he was identified as pastor of the Christian church. Since the communists hated religion and believed pastors to be one of their greatest threats, they murdered him. This disheartening news was received by a letter slipped out of the country weeks after the fact. It seemed as if the enemy was winning.

In spite of this great loss, Jimmy's heart was filled with great concern for the people of his land. His concern for his family hiding in the mountains grew with each passing day. The helplessness he felt by being in America nagged at his conscience. Something had to be done. He expressed this to John on several occasions, and John's heart too was burdened more and more for the boat people. John, by nature, was not one to sit on the sidelines and wait for someone else to make the plays. He felt there must be a way to help these people. Soon he would find out how.

John and Clay Cooper were in Los Angeles for meetings with other missionaries when the idea of trying to obtain a ship to help rescue the boat people came to mind. This ship idea might be the way to move from helplessness to helping. As impossible as it seemed for a common missionary to obtain a ship, John pursued the idea. Finding a ship for such a venture was almost unthinkable. It required knowledge that no one in John's circle had. But in spite of the difficulties, John and Clay felt it was the Lord's idea. It was the love of Christ that compelled John to go on in spite of the odds. It was as big an order to consider obtaining a ship as it to man it and set off to sea to rescue the perishing six thousand miles away. Again a promise from the Word of God came to mind, and John recalled the words of the angel in Luke 1:37: "For nothing will be impossible with God." So he would see if God would do the impossible.

The boat people, knowing they faced near-certain death at sea, were still willing to give up any possessions they had, leave their families, and risk imprisonment and perhaps untold suffering just to get their freedom. The world witnessed before their eyes from 1975–1980 the true conditions of communist Vietnam spoken by the resolve of the people to be willing to leave their homeland and their families for the sake of freedom.

It was early 1978 when Clay and John contacted the organization called Food for the Hungry about the need for a ship to help rescue the Vietnamese people perishing at sea. They, along with other organizations, had the desire to help, but finding a ship to do the job was difficult. There just didn't seem to be anything available anywhere. The plan to get a ship was beginning to look as if it wasn't meant to be.

Just as all hope was beginning to disappear, Jimmy called from Michigan. After one of his meetings at a church a man came up to him and told Jimmy he owned a ship docked in Brisbane, Australia, that might be able to be used for this purpose. This was no coincidence. Jimmy's excitement could not be contained, so he called John immediately in LA. To John this had the familiar ring of answered prayer, and he shared in Jimmy's excitement.

The plan to rescue the boat people was beginning to come together. What started out as a dream was beginning to be seen as a plan from the very heart of God. John made two trips to Australia to see if the ship would be suitable for such a mission. Again, John had no experience in these areas, but he kept in mind that the disciples of Jesus didn't have experience with what they were called to do either. They had simple faith and they helped change the world. He too would act on simple faith and leave the details to the Lord.

Once he got a look at the ship and decided that he wanted it, he had to slip into a new role, that of "wheeler and dealer." He had to buy the ship, find a crew, and care for the details of drydocking and sailing. Negotiating an acceptable price on the ship and such didn't come easily, but he managed to purchase the ship with funds from organizations associated with Jerry Falwell and Billy Graham.

The ship was an old World War II corvette from the Australian Navy, the *SS Akuna*. It was about 200 feet long and had been converted into a yacht. The Australian long-shoremen were not cooperative in the process of getting the ship ready for sea or in helping with the rescue, so John took the ship to Singapore. There he arranged the updating that needed to be done and selected a crew. Most of the crew were not Christians, but all were willing to work hard for the mission, called "Operation Rescue." Every aspect of this mission was something new to John. Taking care of all the details of getting the ship ready for sea was contrary to his random nature, but things did get done—often miraculously.

John's ability to effectively communicate the needs of these people and how they could be helped was used by God to secure the needed financial support for such a mission. People from all over the world helped in Operation Rescue. This was a very expensive operation, and the Lord always provided needed money. Buying the ship, supplying the ship, and paying the crew involved hundreds and thousands of dollars. There was a sense of urgency, as each day that passed meant more lives lost at sea. John believed God would supply all these needs, because he rested in the knowledge that God "is not wishing for any to perish but for all to come to repentance" (2 Peter 3:9). If there were vessels to be used to rescue these people, he thought, the Lord would provide a way to get the job done, for "every beast of the forest is mine, the cattle on a thousand hills" (Ps. 50:10).

Time was wasting as more and more people attempted escape, with most dying as they tried. The Vietnamese had been fleeing the South from the day it fell into the hands of the communists. Every conceivable method of escape was used, but mostly fishing boats. This entailed the risk of trusting unknown sources who were in the business of helping people escape. Unfortunately the world was not much interested in their plight. All the surrounding countries soon had had enough of the Vietnamese refugees. Most of the refugees wanted to come to America, but many would end up in Australia or France.

Most would end up initially in Indonesia. The Indonesian government did not want the burden of these refugees and soon became less than cooperative. They established a policy in 1978 of turning the refugees away. If they had to return to Vietnam, unspeakable horrors awaited them. However, the hope for freedom was deep in the hearts of every refugee. The risk was not too great.

It was an exciting day when they first set out to sea for Operation Rescue in December 1978. With the crew set (most were Indonesian) and a handful of volunteers from Liberty College to help, they ventured from the port of Singapore out into the South China Sea and the Gulf of Siam. They set out on a circular route that would most likely send them in the direction where boats would get lost at sea. Their mission would be to help as many people as possible in the five- to ten-day excursions. Specifically, this meant that when they came across a boat they would first seek to assist that boat in making it safely to shore. Taking people on board would be a last resort. If the people were so much in need of help that their lives were in danger, then they would bring them on board. This was true most of the time.

Soon the dangers became apparent to all. The biggest threat besides the storms was the unpredictable and unfriendly types of people who sailed the same seas. One incident early in Operation Rescue demonstrated this point.

Shortly after the *Akuna* set out to sea, a Malaysian coast guard boat approached the *Akuna* at about midday. John was unaware of the boat approaching because he was in the captain's quarters taking care of some details involving the maintenance of the ship. The coast guard officer brought his boat alongside of the ship and forced his way on board. The ship had done nothing wrong, and it was peculiar to everyone on board that this officer seemed so agitated. He and a few sailors boarded the *Akuna*. The Malaysian officer searched the ship briefly and headed for the ship's cabin. The tension grew as he forced his way into the captain's cabin. John, caught completely off guard by this intrusion, found to his surprise a gun pointed right into his stomach.

Feeling more indignant than fearful at that moment, John began to argue with the Malaysian officer. The arguing escalated until the officer began to back down. It soon became apparent that the officer and his men were looking for money and any other valuables to confiscate, rather than enforcing some law at sea. He got nothing.

Miraculously, the officer decided not to push his case any further and left the cabin to board his own boat. The ship was unarmed, and any violent incident would have ended in tragedy. The crew had no way to defend themselves, and even if they had it would be difficult to prove that the incident was provoked. The Malaysian government also would have prosecuted the crew, and Operation Rescue would have ceased about as soon as it had started. With all these factors in mind, John, treading where angels feared, still told off the officer as he was leaving: "You can come on board anytime to examine our refugees, but don't you ever come on board again and come into the captain's cabin with your gun drawn!"

It was later found out that many of these Malaysian officials had bank accounts in Las Vegas to hoard all the riches that they confiscated from innocent victims at sea and at the ports. For the boat people, their greatest threat was not storms at sea or even engine trouble, but the Thai and other area pirates that lurked in the waters of the South China Sea.

Thai fishermen soon found they could make a lot more money robbing the boat people than fishing the seas. Countless stories emerged of Thai pirates entering boats, beating people, raping the women and young girls, and confiscating their goods. The boats were almost always filled far beyond capacity. The people, weakened by the rough sea, malnourished, and dehydrated, were unable to resist the obvious advantage of the pirates. For a people to endure these unspeakable horrors for the sake of freedom was remarkable.

There were countless stories of the horrors and of the miracles that took place over the thirteen-month period of Operation Rescue. The experience of the Vietnamese can be illustrated by a story related by Clay Cooper, who traveled on one of the rescue missions.

It was the morning of the 19th of June, 1979, and the *Akuna* was located in the South China Sea almost exactly between Singapore and Saigon. The Indonesian captain had spotted what appeared to be a boat on the horizon. It was the beginning of a beautiful morning, with the sun just cresting the sea. But it would go unnoticed as an alert was sounded and the crew was quickly assembled to pursue this image. Sure enough, soon before their eyes were 326 people crammed so close to one another that they could scarcely move. They had not seen such an overcrowded boat as this, and all the boats were overcrowded.

This fishing boat had left the shores of Vietnam eighteen days earlier with two other boats packed just like this one. Within days they had become separated from each other, and this boat had lost one of its engines and was at the mercy of the current and whomever might help. The *Akuna* came alongside the craft and saw for themselves the agony that 326 people had collectively endured for days. For the new observers on the deck this experience was overwhelming. (On almost every trip, observers from around the world from newspapers, volunteer organizations, and Christian organizations would go along to take pictures of the effort.) The faces of joy and desperation were too much to view without being emotionally overcome. The thought of what these people were willing to endure for the glimmer of hope for freedom was stunning.

Ha Jimmy shouted through the hailer to inquire about the condition of the people on board. It was generally the policy to avoid taking people on board the *Akuna* if possible. If they could assist the people by supplying them with more provisions, fix their engines, refuel, or set them in a direction of safety, then they would do that first. This policy allowed the *Akuna* to have a maximum impact as well as stay within the bounds of international law. If people were taken on board, they became the sole responsibility of the ship. This would be unwise because they would not be able to find a country that would settle them. But the response to Jimmy's call was overwhelming. There were so many sick and injured they had to do something. John and the captain quickly conferred and decided that they would allow all the women and children on board, along with the sick and injured. The boat along with the remaining men would be placed in tow after refurbishing their supplies.

Quickly Janis Bernard, the ship's nurse from New Zealand, rushed to prepare powdered milk reinforced with essential vitamins. The scene on deck soon was almost out of control, with mothers and their children being pushed on board faster than the crew could assist them. Miraculously no one was hurt or fell in. The nurse then organized a makeshift medical clinic. Everyone who didn't have a responsibility with the ship's crew was pulled into service to assist with the refugees. Jo and Mary Helen Cooper were among the extras. Untrained people were soon providing relief to scores by applying medicated soaps to injured flesh and giving nourishing food to hungry souls. The nurse treated the more serious injuries first, including a scalded shoulder, ulcerated arm, infected sores, sunburns, and infected insect bites. Luckily there were no life-threatening illnesses that would require more than the ship could provide.

As the day grew on, the heat and humidity began to exhaust the crew. The heat seemed to double on the gray deck. The scorching sun was as much an enemy as the pirates that lurked in the same waters. But once things settled down a bit it became more apparent the kind of conditions these folks had endured for the past eighteen days. Sanitation was near impossible with just two stalls for a makeshift toilet. With the people packed in like sardines, few could avail themselves of them. As the deck filled with refugees it seemed impossible that they had once all been on that one boat. The boat was still crowded with just the men.

The ship had a few shower stalls. The refugees welcomed a shower like it was the most luxurious experience of their lives. The open deck and all spaces below on the open floor became luxurious beds for the weary refugees. But sleep was not the first thing on their minds. Upon having their meal of rice, vegetables, and fish they almost in one accord began to sit cross-legged with pen and paper in hand and write furiously to their loved ones left behind that their fortune was good so far. The *Akuna* would see to it that these letters were mailed when they got back to Singapore. As the sun began to set and the day of rescue was about to end, people began to settle onto the deck floor. They welcomed the steel floor with undisturbed slumber once night fell. They hadn't been able to stretch out their legs in days.

Tarps were spread across the deck to protect people from the direct sun. Clay and John began to walk the deck and extend to the women and children a loving hand or glance of assurance. One couldn't help but see on the faces of the mothers the days of terror they had just endured. They knew that they were risking their own lives and the lives of their children in this escape. A lingering look of sheer fear was in many of their eyes. Upon some inquiry Clay and John learned that this group had already endured a raid by pirates, and several of the girls had been raped. Those haunting, desperate eyes would forever be remembered by John and Jo.

John would walk the deck, stripped down to his pants and tank-top undershirt, to check to see if the refugees' needs were being met. He tried to meet as many people as he could, and he remembers how afraid the children would be at first to see him. After a little time they grew to love him and he couldn't keep them away from him. He loved that.

After a few days they were able to allow the men from the boat in tow to board the ship for awhile. For those who had spouses or children on board it was an exciting reunion.

That morning Clay Cooper began to interview some of the Vietnamese as to how they secured their escape. Many were professional people who gave up everything they had to leave Vietnam.

Representative of many on the boat, Thuy Tran Chau had left his wife and children behind. He left with hopes of establishing residency in some country and then being able to send for his family when he had the money. Tran was a pilot for the South Vietnamese air force and was imprisoned for three and a half years by the communists. He lived on one bowl of rice and a little salt each day. He lost forty pounds while in prison. His wife was given a job for what amounted to $10 a month. His whole family was put in great hardship as a result of this ill treatment. The family was barely able to survive, and life wasn't much better after his release. Escape from Vietnam would be the only way for things to improve.

When he was released he was not allowed to return to his family. Chinese were encouraged to leave the country, so he was able to get a fake ID that said he was Chinese. From there he had to pay 5 ounces of gold to a government agent and 2 ounces of gold to the boat owner. Everyone had to pay the 2 ounces of gold, even the babies. This amounted to more than one person could muster. In most cases several family members gave sacrificially just to get one person out. It was their only hope.

There were literally hundreds of such stories. Now they were safe on the *Akuna*. Well fed and supplied, they would soon reach their destination. That destination was a small island off the shores of Malaysia, chosen by John and the captain as a good place to land so the group could get placed into a refugee camp. They hoped to be discovered by someone within a few days of their landing. It was a risk for the crew of the *Akuna,* because they could run out of fuel, and if they were caught helping the refugees the Malaysian government would likely refuse to assist them. But they calculated the distance to the liter of fuel and decided to go for it.

When it came time to have the refugees reboard the boat it was even more apparent how utterly crowded it had been. This small fishing boat would again become the flotation device for 326 Vietnamese. They boarded at dusk and would float to the nearby island by morning. As Clay observed the process of loading the passengers back on the boat it seemed completely packed, and there were still half the people yet to board. People knelt down and found places in the hull, cramming in like sardines. It seemed an impossibility to get them on, but they did it as they had done before. Clay Cooper compared it to putting a size 12 in a size 5 shoe.

Jimmy, the only Vietnamese-speaking person on board, took the opportunity to lead the people in worship services the few days they were on board. He told them how Jesus had come two thousand years ago to rescue them from an even greater peril than the sea and communist totalitarianism, the oppression of their own sin. He told them that Jesus gave everything He had, including His own life and blood, for them. When Jimmy gave an invitation to receive Christ as their Savior, the response was overwhelming.

After the final gospel service and prayer, they gave each family a New Testament or a gospel of John. Then they directed the boat toward the island they could see in the faint distance. They landed there just as the sun was beginning to break. They rushed ashore and unloaded their provisions, and then a couple of men took the fishing boat back out to the sea and sank it, then swam back to shore. They had to do this or else the government would likely put them back on it and send them somewhere else. They were as safe as they could be now. This was as much as they could possibly hope for, and they knew that the Lord had been with them.

The crew and volunteers of the *Akuna* were exhausted but at the same time full of some of the greatest satisfaction of their lives. They had saved literally hundreds from death and abuse and had given them the light of the gospel. What happened from the island to the point of their placement will never be known for most of the cases. The knowledge that they reached safe shores was enough, and the *Akuna* headed back to Singapore to get ready for another mission.

The day-to-day routine could get boring and tedious. Most days were not filled with rescue operations, but with keeping the ship running efficiently and seeing to the needs of the crew. It was an expensive operation keeping the ship going. There was the fuel, food and water, and the wages of the Indonesian crew. But the Lord provided it all and it demonstrated His love for the desperate people of Vietnam.

On one occasion basic provisions ran out before they could reach port and caused a crisis no one would forget. Fresh water was at a premium on the high seas. The ship was a steam-powered vessel and contained four 12,000-gallon tanks. On one trip steam pipes blew and they lost all the water. Besides the loss of power there was the very real need of providing water to the twenty-two people on board. They needed to be towed to Singapore, but that would take a couple of days, and things were getting desperate. They tested all of the tanks to see if any contained water, and they were all bone-dry. John and his group began to pray for God to provide, taking the Lord at His word in Philippians 4:19, "And my God will supply all your needs according to His riches in glory in Christ Jesus." Two days later John called the first mate and chief engineer to see what he had discovered—that one of the tanks was filled with 12,000 gallons of sweet, undeniably fresh water. The two couldn't believe it, so they took the bolts off the tank to make sure. The captain of the ship seemed unimpressed at first, thinking that the water must be salt water that had come in from some leak in the hull. But upon tasting for himself, he couldn't deny that the water was indeed fresh, and he had no idea how it got there. John knew. I was the Lord Himself, rich in mercy and power. They limped into port, but the members of the missionary crew were rejoicing at the wonderful work of the Lord. They would get the ship ready as soon as possible and set off to rescue more boat people.

There was no predictable pattern to Operation Rescue. Surprises were always around the corner. Once they came across ten nearly starved people on a deserted island. They had been there for two weeks making fires and yelling for help, but nobody came. These boat people were all that remained of a couple of dozen Vietnamese who had soon found out there were no laws at sea. Their boat had been boarded and robbed several times in their journey to freedom. The girls were raped and beaten, and several of the men were murdered. The cruelty of these thugs knew no end. The last band of pirates damaged the boat beyond repair, and it slowly began to sink. Left for dead in the South China Sea, they had managed to reach a small island. All their food was gone, and there was little on the island. As John reported this story he hesitated to go on. He finally decided to explain that when they came upon this group they were as haggard as any he had seen, and their look of horror seemed deeper. After coming to their aid they found out all that had happened to them. In order to survive they were forced to eat the remains of those who were murdered by the pirates or had died. Their rescue by the *Akuna* seemed to be received with a strange combination of terror, joy, and guilt.

This chilling story of cruelty and survival seemed to underscore how necessary Operation Rescue was to the effort to save the boat people. They were witnesses of the very depths of man's sinfulness and the heights of God's mercy to save. Stories such as this one were common.

Operation Rescue went on for thirteen months, saving the lives of at least one thousand souls for whom Christ died. By late 1979 into early 1980 the number of refugees diminished. John and Jo began to see a growing need for better help in the refugee camps rather than the sea rescue mission. This need first came to John's attention when he visited a refugee camp called Sakeo on the Thai-Cambodian border. Sakeo meant "death camp." It got this name because when it first opened, fifty people a day were dying. The Thai government had placed thirty thousand Cambodian refugees in this camp, with very little support. These refugees were fleeing the "killing fields" of the rabidly Maoist group known as the Khmer Rouge. Upon John's visit he saw that the international volunteers were living much like the refugees. They worked twelve-hour days, ate poorly, and had dilapidated living quarters.

John's instinct told him that the best way to meet the needs of the refugees was to make sure that the doctors, nurses, and other volunteers were reasonably comfortable. A burned-out staff would not be able to help anyone. He quickly secured furniture and a cook. This was more than a gesture, because John made sure any refugee effort, as well as any Christian organization, he was involved with should make every effort to keep the staff healthy and comfortable.

This experience led to another ministry for refugees. John's concern for the refugees' ultimate welfare grew. He saw how many were spending months held up in a refugee camp with little progress in getting placement to some new country. The surrounding countries did not care what happened to the mostly Vietnamese refugees. So he felt that he would do what he could to help ensure that these people got out of the camps. He became involved with the Malaysian government agency that dealt with the great influx of Southeast Asian refugees. The government didn't want anything to do with the refugees and was sending them away anytime they could. In fact, all the countries in the Gulf of Siam region had the same policy. The refugees were unwanted everywhere.

The Malaysian government allowed John to enter the Malaysian refugee camp in Pulau Bedong. This had become the dumping ground for about thirty-three thousand people. The paperwork to get someone placed was enormous. John began to work with volunteers from the Red Crescent Society (the Muslim equivalent to the Red Cross).

He and Jo worked out of their base in Kuala Lumpur, a very large and modern city. Their apartment was on the eighth floor, and they had all the comforts of home, with shopping malls and fast-food chains nearby. John became the director for World Concern, a Christian relief organization, in Malaysia. This position gave him authority to manage thirty to forty workers in the refugee camp at Pulau Bedong. Most of John's work involved getting refugees from Vietnam placed into a host country where they could start a new life. In all, he was able to get over nine hundred refugees out of the camp and into a new country.

The administrative work that this involved was something that John had grown to understand and become quite competent in, and of course with the Lord's help, the work was done. John approached this new challenge as he had almost any challenge of his ministry, first seeing the need and asking the Lord for help, and then just doing it. "It has been amazing to see what God has done through me with this approach," he said.

John keenly sensed the need to establish good key relationships to get the job done. This involved getting along with the Muslim Red Crescent organization. They were very concerned that John not proselytize while in the camps. This was a difficult requirement when John's entire being wanted to share the gospel with those desperate people. John managed to get close to several "higher-ups" in the Muslim world, which proved to be very useful in his refugee camp work. When John would make a request for placement, or any other request, it was more likely to be granted because of these key relationships.

Probably the most important relationship he made was with the head of the Red Crescent Society in Malaysia. She was of Chinese descent and was the daughter of a multi-millionaire. She disliked John at first and treated him with contempt. But John in great patience and the love of Christ was able to win her over, and they became friends. She wasn't Muslim and even told John before he returned to the States that she was going to start going back to church.

The Newmans continued this ministry until 1983. Even though he was ordered not to preach to the people, John was often able to share the good news of Jesus dying for them. Both on the ship and at the refugee camps he was able to reap a spiritual harvest. He said, "We tried to make it hard for them to believe. After all, we literally saved their lives. They would do almost anything for anyone in order to be saved. Their gratitude was tremendous. We wanted to make sure that they understood the cost for true belief in Christ." Scores had indicated decisions for Christ through Operation Rescue and the refugee camp work. There is no way to know what happened after they reached their new homes throughout the world, but no doubt many have held on to their faith and demonstrated their gratitude to Christ with obedience to Him.

Chapter 12

I Left My Heart in Vietnam

The crisis of the Vietnamese boat people was fading, and the refugee camps were beginning to thin. The Red Crescent Society was placing restrictions on John and Jo's work in the refugee camp. The doors of opportunity in the camp were closing, and they sensed their usefulness waning. They had fought the good fight and it was time to pull back, so they made arrangements to go home to Spokane in 1983.

Exhausted and still emotionally weary from the events of the past few years, they sought to give themselves time to rest and recuperate completely. As they made their way back to Spokane they knew they could stay with their daughter, Barbara, and her family. Her home had been a safe place in the days after the fall of Vietnam, and they looked forward to time to wind down, a welcome relief from work among the refugees.

The Lord had better things in mind, however. He was going to provide them with their own comfortable home. Clay Cooper's wife, Mary Helen, had passed away in the early 1980s. Clay soon found love again and married a Vietnamese refugee he had met in his service for the Lord. They moved into a house right next door to Clay's house and talked about what to do with the other house. They thought they could either rent it out or sell it for extra income. But they sensed that the Lord wanted them to do something else; they agreed that the Lord wanted them to give the house to John and Jo as a gift. When they called John over to their house one day and announced their intentions, it about knocked John off his feet. It was just like the Lord to bless them in this way, and it was a mighty big gift.

John and Jo were welcome at their daughter's spacious house, but there wasn't anything like having your own home. It was quite a blessing. They humbly accepted and made it a cozy home for themselves and visitors to enjoy. John was well acquainted with the house because he had helped build it for Clay and Mary Helen many years earlier. That made it even more special. John often says that he has had no need for money in all his years of serving the Lord. "Somehow, some way, all our needs have been met. It has been wonderful," he says.

Though they were officially going to retire, that hardly seemed the appropriate term. John had no intention of just sitting around while people in the world hadn't heard the gospel and had a chance to receive the Savior. He asked his mission society for anything that he could do. They gave him the responsibility of promoting mission work in the land of China. China in the early eighties was going through some changes that left the door open to the gospel slightly. Harsh Maoist policies were being modified, and the opportunity for greater freedom was developing. People from the West were beginning to travel to China, and China was inviting Americans to come and teach or perform some other service. Religion had been strictly forbidden in China for decades, but the communist government was relaxing its oppression in that realm as well. All the signs for careful steps toward reaching out to China seemed to be in place, and John was going to go from church to church to share about the new opportunities.

John served in this ambassador role for several months, showing a film on modern China and some of the opportunities there. He was able to encourage Christians all over the country to give money for new projects such as printing Bibles and sending teachers to China. He felt used of the Lord, but he still wanted somehow to reach the people of his heart, the mountain people of Vietnam. He had been involved with some radio programs in the past in hopes that they might be heard. He began to pursue setting up a regular program for the Koho-speaking people and sent out pleas for funding this big operation.

He actually began his radio ministry when he was in Malaysia, but he wanted to provide a consistent program that would reach the Koho people every week with the gospel message, Scripture, and music. John is particularly comfortable before a microphone, likely from making audiotapes to send back to the States when he was in Vietnam. He was able to quickly obtain financing for the expenses of producing the broadcast. John produced it for years by himself, and Jimmy came on board in the late eighties to help him make the broadcasts. Jimmy had settled down in South Carolina with other Vietnamese and mountain people and began a ministry there, so he had to fly out to Spokane about every three months to make the tapes.

John was able to use the studio of KMBI Christian radio in Spokane to produce the programs. With the limited information coming out of Vietnam it was hard to tell what kind of impact they were having, but soon they got word via a few letters that people were flocking to their radios twice a week to hear John and Jimmy's program.

In John's "retirement" years he was still very active in serving the Lord and having a good time. He used to play tennis whenever he could and enjoyed golfing during temperate times of the year. He and Jo made the rounds to churches that had been involved with their support over the years. They became members of Garland Avenue Alliance Church. One of their greatest pleasures was getting together with their friends and family to go out to eat.

Time was catching up with John, however. After visiting the doctor for a regular checkup in 1987 he was told he needed to take a treadmill test. He soon found himself in the operating room having five bypasses performed on his heart. John seemed the least concerned of anybody and came through the surgery with flying colors. His road to recovery was fast, and no one would guess that he was approaching 80 years old. Before word got around that he had open heart surgery he was visiting churches again on Sunday mornings. When anyone would ask how he felt, he would say "never better" and give thanks to the Lord.

All the fun aside, he still maintained his focus on providing some sort of contact and encouragement to the mountain people of the Central Highlands of Vietnam. The radio program served as the best means to do this. Even though it was a one-sided conversation, he knew the Lord was using it to reach thousands of people.

One of John and Jimmy's close friends from the Koho people back in Vietnam was Giao (pronounced jow) Cilpam. He was a young tribal pastor taking on some of the new churches that were born out of the revival. When the communists took over he was hunted down for his "subversiveness" and thrown into prison. He lived on a little rice and water each day for three years before he was released, and was arrested again not long after that. In the late eighties he was released and decided that he had to get out of Vietnam. He wanted to take his wife, but couldn't, so he came out himself with the help of many Vietnamese and tribal residents in the U.S. It was quite a story in itself. He joined the team of John and Jimmy in the broadcast booth shortly after he came to the U.S. His next goal was to raise the money for his wife to get out. It took several years and several thousand dollars in cash to bribe her way out of Vietnam and join Giao. They were finally able to get her out in 1995.

The format of the radio program is unique. At the KMBI studio one will hear the Christmas tune "Joy to the World" played every half hour when the John, Jimmy, and Giao team is at work. "Joy to the World" is the theme song for the program. Program manager Gary Leonard couldn't believe his ears at first, but when John explained how this song has special meaning to the mountain people, he understood.

> *Joy to the world, the Lord is come!*
> *Let earth receive her King;*
> *Let every heart prepare Him room,*
> *And Heaven and nature sing,*
> *And Heaven and nature sing,*
> *And Heaven and Heaven, and nature sing.*

These were words that meant so much to the Montagnards, along with the verses that follow.

Following the theme song comes a short prayer and a Scripture reading in the Koho language. Every word is in Koho. Although neighboring tribes don't speak Koho, they are able to understand much of it. In God's sovereign plan He is able to use this one language to reach thousands with the message of salvation through Christ. Every effort is made to produce a quality program. It's John's job to read the Scripture because he, interestingly, speaks the language more accurately than his colleagues. They will usually have some music planned and then John and Jimmy do a little joking around about old times. The program attempts to cover all generations so that there is no generation gap. After the affectionate banter between John and Jimmy, Giao takes over with a sermonette, usually lasting about fifteen minutes. He's an old-time preacher in many ways—takes every message right out of the Bible and pours his heart out.

Often he has no prepared message, and yet it is outstanding in quality. John says he is amazed almost every time Giao speaks. He speaks with such authority and passion. The three men provide some sort of conclusion and end the program with music.

They prepare forty half-hour programs every three months, all within a week's time. The cost of these recordings and their broadcasting runs about $7,000 for a three-month time. It's a very exhausting schedule, but very rewarding. After the tapes are made, they are shipped out to the Philippines in Manila and are broadcast into Vietnam by Far East Broadcasting Company, a Christian radio ministry in the Philippines. They are broadcast during the prime-time hours on Thursday and Sunday evenings. John knows that listeners like to hear from the old guy who hasn't forgotten them. They receive a few letters out of Vietnam from mountain people, and they often mention how the program encourages the believers and serves to instruct the people. One of the great needs of the thousands of new believers since the fall of Vietnam has been to train leaders in the Bible. The Vietnamese government would simply not allow it.

According to all indications, the revival of 1972 is still bearing fruit to the tune of an estimated 94,000 new believers in the tribal lands of Da Lat and Ban Me Thuot. It could easily be spreading beyond those areas as well. The Da Lat area has an estimated 100,000 believers total, and the Ban Me Thuot region has about 140,000 believers. All these people are in great need of New Testaments and trained leaders. The radio program helps fill some of this gap, but it is not a substitute for direct training. The Holy Spirit has guided these pastors and leaders in spite of their lack of official Bible training.

A few years ago John heard of the need for transistor radios in the tribal areas of Vietnam. Before long he was getting the word out about this need, and soon hundreds of radios were delivered so that people could continue to listen to Christian radio programs like John's. He'll do anything within his power to help those people.

The radio ministry has been the heart of what John and Jo have been involved in since their return from Malaysia. It is very rewarding, because it keeps them deeply involved with the mountain people. It's a perfect thing to do with circumstances as they are, being up in years, and most of all being separated by six thousand miles. The simple pleasures of life have filled the time between tapings. They enjoy life to the fullest, but John still lives by the old adage, "Only one life, 'twill soon be past, only what's done for Jesus will last," so he does all that he can to be used of the Lord. He also knows a lot of the work now is being done by the younger generation, often with a different strategy than his village evangelism approach. He often voices his concern that the burden for world missions is not as strong as it once used to be, that perhaps there are not enough Christians willing to serve the Lord on the mission field. He sees that much of our energy seems to be spent within our own churches and our own problems. He wonders if some of these problems might go away if we were more willing to help others around the world with much more serious problems. He greatly desires to see willing young Christians know what an exciting life it is to be a missionary and to make their living by serving the Lord.

Besides the radio program, John sends out monthly news-letters through OC International and keeps up correspondence with dozens of people around the country who continue to support his ministry in money and in prayer. John and Jo also make a special effort to reach out during the Christmas season with a myriad of cards. One of their greatest blessings is getting cards in return. One card in particular is a special blessing. It comes from Southern California from a family they rescued out of the South China Sea in 1979. A few years ago John and Jo were traveling through Southern California and had a reunion with that family. Jo, with teary eyes, told how when they got to the door and opened it, the family cried their eyes out in joy and thanksgiving. They shared a meal together that night and talked about each other's lives and what the Lord was doing. It stands out as one of their life's greatest moments. They hear from them every year, and each year's card is a treasure like no other.

It wasn't long before dramatic changes in the world would change the rules on how we relate to one another and who we call our friend or our foe. Right before our eyes in 1989 we saw the Berlin Wall come tumbling down, and along with it the entire communist bloc of Europe. The end of the Cold War had seemed an impossibility just a few years earlier, but the cloud of nuclear destruction that loomed over the world's head for decades was all of a sudden lifted. Those events changed the world in just a few months' time. It was incredible.

However, the events in Europe and the former Soviet Union did not spread to the Asian communist bloc. China, Vietnam, North Korea, Laos, and Cambodia were all put on the defensive by these events, and modifications would be inevitable but slow. China had already begun to loosen up, but the world saw the limitations to freedom that the communist regime would tolerate at the Tiananmen Square Massacre. Vietnam was little affected by these events, but they too were beginning to see that the policies of strict socialism were dragging the country into bankruptcy and hunger. They began to allow the residents of Ho Chi Minh City (Saigon) to engage in some free enterprise, and this has expanded little by little to all parts of the country.

The government of Vietnam began to see the need to come out of isolation and join the world once again. It needed money, and eventually it would need to mend fences with its old enemy the United States. The Vietnamese have begun to expand their tourist business, and new hotels are being built all over the country in anticipation of a huge tourist business. In the city of Da Lat alone they have built a 36-hole golf course and several hotels, one being fifty stories high.

By the end of 1996 the United States and Vietnam had established a full diplomatic relationship. This change in policy would open more doors for traveling back to Vietnam. As early as 1994 John was planning to make a return trip to Vietnam. It was the desire of his heart to go back and see the people he had once ministered to and to see the people he has been talking to via radio all these years.

As there began to be some limited travel to Vietnam, many folks who once served there wanted a chance to go back. Two Christian and Missionary Alliance missionaries went back to Vietnam and tried twice to travel up from Saigon to tribal land in the Central Highlands, even though they were told they couldn't by the communist government. Unfortunately they were quickly thrown out of the country. This incident created a greater mistrust on the part of government officials toward former missionaries traveling freely in Vietnam. In another incident a nondenominational group went back in the eighties specifically to attempt a counter-revolution against the communists by using the tribal people. This plot was quickly found out and set the tone for mistrust of church people.

John didn't want to make these kinds of mistakes and jeopardize future possibilities for ministry and, more importantly, the lives of the mountain people. He began talks with several people about the possibility of his returning to Vietnam. Excitingly, at every turn there seemed to be encouragement and open doors.

One of his first contacts was with the National Academy of Scientists, where he knew the president of the organization. John had the idea of turning the old, abandoned medical clinic into an agricultural technical school for the mountain people. The NAS thought this was a great idea for helping the Vietnamese and mountain people as well as getting a way back to Vietnam. They were aware of the fact that since the communist takeover the tribal people have had a difficult time feeding their people off the land, and they wanted to help. John hoped that this would be positively received by the Vietnamese government, since it would help the people and perhaps their economy. For months this plan seemed to be moving forward, but due to politics and funding problems it has yet to be a reality. John still hopes that this might come to pass and that he might have some part in it. He knows that with his language skills he could serve as a good mediator between the English-speaking and tribal-speaking people.

The Lord seemed to have other plans for John, and so he began to look for other open doors. One of his greatest concerns was to get the Word of God into the hands of the tribal people. They loved to sing more than any other group he has heard on earth, so he wanted to get some hymnals into their hands as well.

With the help of some translators he was able to secure computer disks with the entire New Testament in the Koho, Rade, and Juri languages, and a hymnal in Koho. His dream was to go to Vietnam and make thousands of copies of each for the tribal people at a Saigon print shop. This posed a considerable challenge with the government dead set against allowing Christianity to flourish. The computer disks and transcripts sat for months in his basement office, waiting for the contents to be released. John would sit and point to the briefcase, saying, "The communists don't know the power that exists in that briefcase. It is the very power of God. God is in that briefcase and they are afraid of it."

John had been reading in Isaiah 31:3 where the words seemed to fit the challenge of going up against the communist Vietnamese government: "Now the Egyptians [Vietnamese] are men and not God, and their horses are flesh and not spirit." He saw this as God telling him that the obstacles that the communist government might put in the way were no match for God's will.

John's plans to return to Vietnam seemed to develop rapidly. He went to New York to meet the Vietnamese United Nations ambassador in the spring of 1995. Unfortunately that meeting never took place. Relations between the U.S. and Vietnam seemed to yo-yo every week. The past few years had been filled with frustrating plans to go and then doors being shut. For John and Jo it taught them to rely on His timing and to "wait upon the Lord." Everywhere he turned, people were interested in helping establish some kind of work in Vietnam. Even Franklin Graham, son of Billy Graham, showed considerable interest in setting up a medical mission for the tribal people.

John and Jo had set several dates for their possible departure to Vietnam. The very possibility of returning to their people filled them with a childlike excitement. Their senses were filled with the wonder of actually going back and seeing their brothers and sisters in Christ for the first time in over twenty years. They called travel agents, set dates, and set up visa arrangements for the travel. It seemed that each time they set a date it got pushed back for one reason or another.

One day upon my arriving to interview John, he had just five minutes earlier received notification that his visa was not going to be granted by the Vietnamese government. He was stunned. According to John's research this was unprecedented in regard to recent requests for travel. Though he was deeply disappointed, he knew deep down that it was the Lord. He didn't want to submit to the idea that he wasn't going to be able to go, at least for now. He had set several dates, and every time, something came up to stop them. It was time to consider the reality that they would never return. This most current departure date had seemed the most likely to happen, because everything up to that point was going so well. They had heard that traveling was more and more open and that they would probably be able to go to Da Lat and see several people. Now all of a sudden that dream was shattered.

Only a few days after getting word of his visa being denied, John heard from a very reliable source out of Vietnam that in reality it was not safe to travel in Vietnam. He learned about one recent visitor to Da Lat who was tracked step by step by the secret police. The visitor wasn't harassed, but as soon as he left the country every person that he had contact with was visited by the secret police. The secret police intimidated them, and some were beaten. John knew there was a reason for this turn of events and saw how the Lord was protecting them.

After months and months of proclaiming he was going to go back to Vietnam, he had come to the conclusion that he and Jo would not go. It was too risky. His dream of boarding that flight to Saigon and the loving embraces he imagined they would have upon greeting their old friends was gone. They dreamed the impossible and it was just weeks away from reality, with all the signs saying go, and now it looked like he and Jo would have to wait until glory before having their reunion. It was a difficult pill to swallow, but he knew it was the will of God.

John is rarely deeply discouraged, and it didn't take long to formulate plan B. That plan was to send just one person for whom it might be safer. Jimmy's ministry board wouldn't let him go because they thought it would be too risky. And it likely was. Because of Jimmy's previous connections with the South Vietnamese military and the American CIA, he would be a definite target for some kind of harm. The very future of establishing good relations with the Vietnamese government and the possibility of future ministry in Vietnam was at stake. An international incident could sour those opportunities for years to come.

Ha Johnny, Jimmy's brother in California, decided to make the trip. His Vietnamese was better than anyone else, and he didn't have the reputation in communist circles that Jimmy or John had developed. Johnny called his sister in Da Lat four times to discuss his coming and what he could and could not do. His brother-in-law would come down to Saigon and meet Johnny when he arrived. Plans were quickly put into place. John wanted to go more that he could possibly admit, but his love for his brothers and sisters in Christ was greater than the fulfillment of one of his desires.

John had been collecting thousands of dollars for this trip over the years. It would cost approximately $2.50 to print one New Testament. The door was open just a bit in Vietnam to print the New Testaments. The National Church of Vietnam had been granted permission to print thirty thousand in Vietnamese just a few months earlier through the United Bible Society.

The details of Johnny's trip moved along smoothly, and his departure was planned for January 1997. The trip was an expensive venture in terms of dollars, but could reap unbelievable spiritual rewards if they could pull it off. Recent news out of tribal land was exciting. The number of souls coming to Christ was staggering. They heard from just one pastor, who was pastor of several of the tribal village churches, that they had baptized 329 new believers in the past year. He told John and Jimmy that many other pastors were experiencing the same kind of growth among the tribal folks. This pastor, who needs to go unnamed, attributes the success of evangelism to the continued impact of the 1972 revival and the faithfulness to Christ of the believers in the midst of difficult times. This underscored the need for New Testaments and some sort of training for the young and inexperienced pastors trying to feed their growing flocks.

Huan, a tribal pastor, has taken on the ministry of providing a quick training course for some of these pastors.

This intensive training takes place over just four days, and then the pastors are sent back to their villages and a new group returns for training. It's quick and dirty, but seems to be effective.

Another evangelist, a Vietnamese missionary to the tribal people, reported that he had a church leaders training session mixed with an evangelistic outreach. The surprising results were that 278 people came to the Savior Jesus Christ. This same man reported that almost eight hundred people received the Lord just in the months of March and April of 1997. In reality, the number of people coming to faith in Jesus in the tribal lands of Vietnam is phenomenal. The Holy Spirit is still being poured out upon these humble people of the mountains of Vietnam. Though their life here on earth is difficult and uncertain, they are exchanging their animism and demon worship for the worship of the Most High God.

This movement of God can't be blamed on ethnocentric Westerners trying to impose their religion on primitive people. This is clear, because Westerners are simply not there. It is without a doubt the work of Christ Himself through the surrendered souls of the tribes. John is content and excited to have been a part in sowing the seeds of this tremendous spiritual harvest. He says, "Christ said He would build His church, and the gates of hell shall not prevail against it. That sure seems to be happening in Vietnam today."

As preparations were made for Johnny's trip to Vietnam in January 1997 he continued to stay in contact with people inside the country to see if it was still safe. He kept getting the green light, and soon found himself in the air on his way back to his homeland. He carried with him close to $40,000 in cash, a pretty risky thing in itself. He needed the extra cash in order to bribe officials and other key people to let him copy the New Testaments.

As they were able to communicate with people in the region of Da Lat and Ban Me Thuot, they discovered another practical need: motorcycles. So Johnny had enough money to purchase motorcycles for two traveling pastors. The motorcycles would make it easier for them to travel from village to village and to visit more people with less effort. It was an amazing mission, and all was accomplished, yet not without risk.

It was immediately evident that Johnny's presence had not gone unnoticed. He had made plans to stay with a Vietnamese official in the Saigon police department whom he knew in the old days as a friend in Da Lat. Though this seemed to be a friendly contact, it also served as a way for the secret police to keep an eye on all of Johnny's activities. He was followed everywhere by two men. He even began to talk to them and in fact was able to bribe them for the opportunity to print the New Testaments in the language of the tribal people. Johnny wasn't able to go to Da Lat to see his friends and relatives, but some of them came down to Saigon to see him. He was there only a couple of weeks and was able to accomplish everything he and John had hoped for.

When Johnny returned he gave a full report to John, and they praised the Lord for all of His mercy. Everything went according to plan, and as far as they knew, the people that Johnny had contact with were not harassed. It was a tremendous answer to prayer. John had to use most of his radio broadcast money for the mission and was approaching a need of $7,000 by the end of February 1997. He prayed for this need to be met, and the Lord came through, as John knew He would. Money came rolling in for the new set of broadcasts just in time. John knew that the Lord loved these people even more than he did, and it showed time and time again. Even though he couldn't go to Vietnam himself, he still had a satisfaction that only comes from abiding faith in the Lord Jesus Christ.

This has been only a portion of the life of John and Jo Newman. Much more could be written about the work of

God in their lives as His faithful servants—extraordinary lives in so many ways. Together they have touched the lives of literally thousands of people. Together they have help saved the lives of thousands of people. Together they have planted, watered, and reaped the harvest of thousands of souls for Christ. They took the message, the simple story of Jesus Christ, to people who had never heard the name, and established His church.

Are they extraordinary people? Yes, but only in what they have done. They are extraordinary because both of them, without hesitation, time and time again took God at His word and obeyed. It's that simple. They were called and they responded; they were sent and they went. But most of all they loved. Loved first of all Jesus Christ, who died and rose again for them. Loved the people whom Christ had put into their lives. Loved enough to tell everyone that they loved Jesus. Loved so much that they risked their lives to enter a war zone just to tell people of the salvation that was possible through Christ. Loved so much that they found a way to rescue boat people destined to death. Loved so much that at the end of their lives they continue to pray and work for the salvation of the mountain people of Vietnam.

In many ways they are simple, ordinary people. That's why their story needs to be told, to show each Christian who might read these pages what God can do through just one surrendered, obedient soul. If only we could be at the end of our lives and look back with such satisfaction at how we spent our lives. I know that John and his soul mate, Josephine, will hear the words from their Savior, "Well done, My good and faithful servant." Will we?

Epilogue

F olks bundled up for the cold January weather gathered at Garland Avenue Alliance Church for the Saturday afternoon memorial service. Jody and I took a seat and quietly greeted old acquaintances who sat around us. John Newman had slipped out of this world and into the full presence of the Lord on January 19, 2009. I sat thinking about his life and how much he enjoyed serving the Lord, and how he never put a limit on that service. I never met a man who so truly took God at His word without hesitation.

Glenn Johnson began his message with the perfect phrase out of the first chapter of the gospel of John: "There came a man sent from God, whose name was John." The words so eloquently summarized his life and honored him among the saints of old. Although the service gave great honor to his life, it would fall short of tapping into the profound impact this one man had on the eternity of thousands to whom he was sent.

On November 4, 2002, the love of John's life, his friend and partner Jo, died. I knew this would take a considerable amount of wind out of his sails. Though he missed her with all his heart he made the adjustment remarkably well. He remained in their home and became pretty self-sufficient with the help of his friends and family. Shortly after Jo's death John remarked to his daughter, "I still have a ministry," meaning the radio broadcasts to the Koho in Vietnam. He also meant that his life, though in the latter years, was still going to be used of God, and that kept him going.

One of the things I liked most about John was how active he was in several different areas of his life all the time. Though he was deeply spiritual, he was a very normal guy. He consumed the news with an interest in politics and world affairs. He visited Stroh's Fitness Center regularly every week for years, right up to just months before his passing. Now, we're talking a ninety-year-plus guy walking into a fitness center to lift weights and work the machines. I can only hope. He loved watching sports and weighing in on his view of our Northwest pro teams the Mariners, Sonics, and Seahawks. John and his sister Dorothy became inseparable in the latter years. They spent hours together watching baseball, basketball, and football games. If they couldn't be together they would be on the phone with each other, fully analyzing each inning or quarter. They had a blast.

My visits to John became less frequent after doing the research for this book, but I saw him at least twice a year. I would call and make an appointment, and on the other end of the line I would get a low, gruff, and not-so-happy-sounding "Hello?" and I would say, "John, this is Marty." In a whole new tone, he would say "Marty!" in an enthused, affectionate way that I can still hear as clear as day. It was so like John—gruff and manly, and yet as tender as a new shoot of grass. We would often talk of an upcoming taping session with Giao and Jimmy. It was the highlight of his life to have a reunion with the guys every three months and spend an intense week up at KMBI radio making the tapes. Gary Leonard became so committed to the ministry that, though retired, he has maintained the work of producing the broadcasts to the Koho even since John's passing.

Giao and Jimmy continue to come to Spokane every three months to share the Word, song, and their hearts to the tribal people of the Central Highlands. In recent years, there has been some contact with the mountain people, and the church there continues to grow. The growth in large part is due to the faithfulness of the weekly primetime broadcasts. The latest report out of Vietnam indicated that their radios were wearing out and there was a need for new ones. This speaks to the hunger that still exists to hear His Word and receive the encouragement that the broadcasts bring. My hope and that of OC International is that you have been inspired by John and his life and that through your gifts we can ensure that the broadcasts continue for many years to come. We can all be a part of continuing what John, through Christ, began.

If you would like to financially support the radio broadcasts to Vietnam, you may send donations to OC International, PO Box 36900, Colorado Springs, CO 80936, designating your gift for the broadcasts; or, give online at www.onechallenge.org. Donations to OC International are tax-deductible, and you will receive a receipt.

John Newman, 1915-2009

About OC International

OC International is an interdenominational mission agency committed to the vision of healthy churches working together to reach all nations. With more than 400 missionaries worldwide, OC is involved in life transformation, leadership training, evangelism and discipleship, church planting, and sports ministry. OC ministry is contextualized to the needs of those they serve, emphasizing partnership with host-country Christian leaders. For more information, see www.onechallenge.org, or call (800) 676-7837.

Breinigsville, PA USA
28 October 2009
226560BV00001B/2/P